Muslims Call Him Isa,
Some Call Him Savior

Muslims Call Him Isa, Some Call Him Savior

PULLING BACK THE SPIRITUAL VEIL OF RECONCILING MUSLIMS AND CHRISTIANS

Don A Heckman

ISBN-13: 9780692512067
ISBN-10: 0692512063

Table of Contents

(Note: "Isa" is Arabic for "Jesus.")

Introduction

Christ Loves My Muslim Friend

This book's emphasis is simple and yet charged with the challenge that Christ already loves Muslims. What a new thought this might be for those Christians who have rarely had the joy to live out Christ's love in practical terms! Intertwined with Christ's love is my friendship with individual Muslims. To learn to effectively evangelize Muslims, we must love Muslims as friends. Most Christians have very few non-Christian friends, among whom still fewer are Muslim.

Over the last few years, two realizations have shaped my thinking concerning Muslims. *First, the reason more Muslims have not come to Christ is because no one has told them about the Lord.* It isn't fair to look upon a sea of Muslims and conclude that they have all rejected Christ and the Gospel.

In fact, Muslims are more open to the Gospel than ever before. More Muslims have come to Christ in the last fifteen years than in all the years since the death of Muhammad. The Kabyles in Algeria, for example, have come to Christ by the tens of thousands simply because someone told them about the Lord.

Second, my thinking was rocked when a strategist told me that the secret to reaching Muslims was "hordes." We need to send out these "hordes" to do the task remaining of reaching 1.25 billion Muslims. Preparing hordes of solid workers requires training, strategy, and the help of many more supporters who encourage such missionaries from their home churches.

Of course, achieving the task of reaching Muslims through such "hordes" of laborers requires both "senders" and "goers." And senders and goers both need to embrace new ways of thinking that keep the Gospel from being denuded of its intense power. Explaining some of these new ways of thinking is one goal of this book.

In Luke 10:2, Jesus called upon His missionary laborers to pray for more fellow workers in the harvest, as "the harvest truly is great, but the laborers are few." As we see in Luke 10, members of the missionary group were to go "armed" with prayer for other workers for one precise reason: to plant seeds. Our goal is not just the salvation of Muslims, but that each Muslim convert will become another generation aflame for global evangelism. Muslim converts are our seeds for further outreach into the harvest. It is vital that the white-hot power of God be unleashed through the conversion of Muslims, who can then reach, as hordes of their own, into the world of still more Muslims, whom Christ already loves.

My prayer is that the reading of this book will not only instruct us about new ideas for evangelization, but will also open us to see our prejudices so we can deal with our own baggage, impediments, and, frankly, our own limited view of the Gospel. Having a clear understanding of the Gospel is essential because the Gospel is the power of Christ to make us "wise unto salvation in Jesus Christ" (2 Tim. 3:15).

I have intentionally avoided making this book into an academic work. My purpose is to offer seminal ideas and examples, all of which are based on the clear thinking of many servants and workers in the Muslim world.

CHAPTER 1

Test Your Knowledge of Islam

Before we learn how to address Islam, let's test our knowledge of Islam. Circle "True" (T) or "False" (F) for each of these controversial statements to test your knowledge of Islam. To keep your score valid, please refrain, as much as possible, from guessing. When you are done, feel free to debate your answers with others who have had experience with Muslim church planting. Do they agree?

1. T F Muslims believe Jesus is the Messiah.
2. T F Muslims are quiet and unwilling to talk about their faith.
3. T F The Muslim God, Allah, is a totally different God than the Christian God.
4. T F Muslims have resisted the Gospel for centuries.
5. T F Islam is the way of peace.
6. T F Islam and Christianity have many similarities.

7. T   F   Muslims believe in the Ten
            Commandments.

Let's check the answers.

1. *True.* Jesus's Arabic name is Isa al-Masih, or
   Jesus the Messiah. This is how Muslims know
   him. For Christians, this belief is a huge point
   of entry into the lives of Muslims. In the same
   way that "messiah" is defined in Hebrew,
   the Arabic "*massiah*" means "anointed one
   who was sent of God." This is why Muslims
   think of Jesus as a prophet, like Muhammad,
   who was also "sent of God." However, they
   don't see Jesus as God Himself, because for
   a Muslim, it is shameful that a man, Jesus,
   could equate Himself with God.

2. *False.* Muslims are very willing to talk about
   their faith. Some Christians will say, "My
   faith is very personal and private," but it is
   often not so among Muslims. To Muslims,
   faith is public and communal, not personal,
   private, or hidden. Muslims will willingly
   talk about their faith, which is a living submission to obedience that, for them, is never
   separated from their daily lives.

3. *False.* Allah is the Arabic word for "God," just
   as "*dieu*"is the French word for God. When a

non-Christian swears and says, "God!" he or she is not using the name of a different god, but that person certainly does not necessarily know the revelation of who God really is. So it is with Muslims. Also, almost all Arab Christians (fifteen to twenty-five million) call God "Allah." The Arabic-language Bible also uses the word "Allah" for God throughout.

4. *False.* Actually, most Muslims have not even heard of the Gospel. As stated later on, North African Christianity in 125 AD mainly consisted of theological debate in the Latin language. Saint Augustine was one of the greatest debaters during this time. Even though he was a half Kabyle-Berber Algerian, he preferred to work in Latin, a language only spoken by a small, educated class. The first organized church-planting teams among Muslims did not take place until 1985.

5. *False.* Islam is not a way of peace, though Muslims insist that it is. Peace to a Muslim is when each neighborhood, each town, every city and nation, and indeed when the whole world belongs to Islam. Many Muslims are peaceful—most are, in fact. However, Islam, when practiced strictly according to the Koran, is harsh to wives, to unbelievers, and to those

who don't convert to Islam. Most Muslims are more peaceful than their own Koran.

6. *True.* Islam and Christianity have many similarities. Both Muslims and Christians are monotheists. Both groups believe in fasting and giving to charity. Both believe in demons and angels. Both believe in heaven and hell. Both believe the Bible is a holy book. And both believe in the return of Christ, although Muslims believe Muhammad is greater than Christ.

7. *True.* Muslims do believe in the Ten Commandments. People of Jewish faith also believe in the Ten Commandments. For Christians, believing in the Ten Commandments means to receive God's grace in Christ, so that we can embrace these commandments of love with His Spirit at work in us. For Muslims or Jews, however, believing in the Ten Commandments means to accept that the Torah, or the first five Old Testament books, came from God. Muslims believe that the Torah and all of the Old Testament are sacred books from God.

Challenge: "Peace" for Muslims is similar to the Old Testament meaning of the "Shalom," the peace of God. It is the active, penetrating, expanding, and conquering peace of the reign of God on earth. Peace in the Old Testament is not a calm or a quiet moment; it is a victory over darkness.

Question: If the Muslim view of peace is when each town and family is Islamic, what can we learn about the reality of God's peace in the world for Christians today?

Case Study 1
Kamil, a Muslim Friend
Whom God Loves

Let me tell you about a Muslim who was converted as he read the Bible.

Kamil tells his story as follows:

During my childhood and early teen years, I carried my grandfather's vision of spreading the faith of Islam throughout Africa. And I desired to strengthen the Muslim-revival group he founded. I was also burdened, at that time, to translate the Koran into my local language. I was solid in these commitments and would always miss school classes whenever they interfered with Friday prayers at the mosque.

The Dreams Begin

My supernatural dreams first began during primary school. It was 1987. I was in the habit of praying each night before sleep...praising Allah, thanking

Him, and continually asking for guidance from Him. After some time of meditation and prayer, Allah spoke to me in a dream. ["Allah" is the Arabic word for God.]

I knew nothing about the contents of the Bible, but what I saw in my dream was very similar to what is recorded in the book of Acts in the Injil. ["Injil" means "New Testament" or "Gospels" in Arabic.]

This is what I read: "The disciples of Christ were looking intently up into the sky as he was going, when suddenly two men dressed in white stood beside them. 'Men of Galilee,' they said, 'why do you stand here looking into the sky? This same Jesus, who has been taken from you into heaven, will come back in the same way you have seen him go into heaven'" (Acts 1:10, NIV).

In my first dream, I was surprised to see clouds gathering on top of a mountain. After the clouds gathered, two angels dressed in white robes stood on top of the mountain. Jesus was standing between the angels. He left the angels and came to where I stood watching. As He approached me, I knelt down, and He laid His hands on my head. With the deep love I felt from Him, I began repenting. The dream was so powerful to me, but in the morning I told no one for fear of what my family may do to me. I remained silent for that year, telling no one what I had experienced.

Kamil came to Christ and is now mighty in God. Guess what? Kamil, who now lives in Minnesota, wrote me an e-mail this week. Here is my reply.

Kamil,

Thanks for writing. I will of course try to answer some of your questions.

Q: What strategy is working in France?

A: Clearly, you need to invite yourselves into Muslim homes. Second, you need to raise up home groups that mix MBBs (Muslim-background believers in Christ) as well as Muslim seekers. Third, you need to allow Muslims to maintain their Muslim culture and worship style when they come to Christ. Fourth, you need mercy ministries that care for the physical needs of Muslims. Fifth, you need to teach the Bible to Muslims before they are converted, even while greatly showing respect for the Koran. You need to pray for Muslims, for their healing, for freedom from evil spirits, even before they convert.

Q: And what has not been working in the past or what mistakes have been made?

A: What doesn't work is putting seeking Muslims or converted Muslims into a Western church. How do you mix time-conscious Westerners with relationship-sensitive Muslims? How do you mix low levels of hospitality with the great hospitality of the North Africans? Our greatest mistake in France has been this one thing: ignoring their hospitality. Muslims are more open to God than most French or Western people, but few know this, and still fewer people act upon this.

Still, the greatest mistake is that Christians in France, as in most Western countries, separate religious experience and secular life. Muslims rightly reject this form of Sunday-only religious commitment. If Jesus is Lord of all, then He is Lord of our business, our marriages, and so on. This is another key.

Q: How many Muslims are in France, and where is the majority coming from?

A: France has a population of sixty million. Of that, 12 to 15 percent are Muslims. Most are from Algeria, Morocco, Tunisia, Senegal, Mali, Turkey, and Mauritania, in that order.

God is the strength to our lives. Thanks so much for that, Kamil.
Blessings,
Don

Questions for the Reader

1. Given that many Christians feel saved by confessing a phrase, would you accept a Muslim convert as genuine if that person adhered to Jesus but did not use confession? Write your response below.

2. A Muslim who reads a Bible story may be asked what the passage says about God/Allah. Is this Muslim qualified to respond, because he is a Muslim?

CHAPTER 2

Adopting a Person, a Family, a People

My wife, Evey, and I prepared ourselves and our home to receive our first baby boy many months before his birth. Our hearts were enlarged with joy, even before our first child was born. We knew that the changes in our marriage would not be considered a sacrifice in adopting this new person into our lives.

In the same way that our hearts were enlarged with the anticipation of our new child, Paul said in 2 Corinthians 6:11, "O Corinthians, our mouth is open to you, our heart is enlarged." He even used birthing terms in another passage: "My little children, of whom I travail in birth again, until Christ be formed in you" (Gal. 4:19).

Paul not only had the same heartfelt feelings toward the Corinthians that we have toward our children, but he also felt the same labor pains while bringing them to life in Christ! In other words, Paul completely adopted the Corinthians as his own family.

Opening ourselves to Muslim people starts with this same adoptive attitude: with the attitude that, incredibly, Muslims are now part of our extended family.

It is not only possible but also essential to have a passion for the Muslim people we want to know and to reach on behalf of Christ. It is no secret that I am emotionally and spiritually excited when I see a Muslim. God has opened to my wife and me hearts of compassion. We feel caring impulses comparable to the feelings we experience upon seeing a family member whom we've missed for a long time. However, do we have the right to become emotional over a human being we don't even know? Don't people need to prove themselves to you and to me before they are counted as friends?

"Passion before track record" is how God implants His love for Muslims in our hearts

Clearly, you don't wait until a newborn baby proves himself or herself to you before you hold that baby in your arms. Otherwise, the baby would starve first.

"Passion before track record" is how God implants His love for Muslims into our hearts. And it's biblical! "But God showed His love for us, in that while we were yet sinners, Christ died for us" (Rom. 5:8). Thus, God's passion for us (or our passion for Muslims) goes before a superslick track record. Muslims don't have to prove themselves to me before I care for them and adopt them as part of my family so that in turn they can be adopted into Christ's family.

Challenge: Not all Muslims come to Christ as a result of a coach's passion and acceptance of Muslims. Other avenues for Muslims to genuinely come to Christ include apologetics, proof texts, or even monetary improvement. Christians also sometimes have mixed motives in coming to Christ.

Question: If a Muslim comes to Christ without an accepting and caring Christian to assist, a Christian who has a passion for these people of Abraham, what are the possible consequences for the newly converted Muslim's future productivity in the kingdom of God?

Case Study 2
Ahmed, a Muslim Friend Whom God Loves

Ahmed had a family of six children in Algeria. His wife announced to him early one morning that she was pregnant with his seventh child. Ahmed was already partially paralyzed on his left side. He couldn't till the soil and work the fields due to his paralysis. That meant that he couldn't possibly feed and provide for a seventh child in addition to the other six.

Ahmed couldn't bear this shame. In fact, the shame was so great that Ahmed decided at once to commit suicide. Ahmed took a pistol with him to a coffee bar, where he decided to drink his last coffee. When he finished the espresso, he put the cup down and prepared to shoot himself.

However, things didn't go as planned. By God's grace, a Christian with a baffling background came into the coffee bar. He was a man like Jonah of the Old Testament, unwilling to serve God but doing it anyway. This reluctant Christian said to God, "OK, I'll take these Gospels of Luke to this coffee bar, though it is probably for a lost cause!" (We've since met this "former Jonah," who is now a zealot for Christ.)

The Jonah-like Christian gave Ahmed a Gospel of Luke and left. Ahmed read part of the story of the prodigal son. This is the story of the Jewish father who was shamed but still loved his son. Ahmed trembled. He went home. His wife cried for joy because she saw that Ahmed was still alive; he hadn't followed through with his plan.

Ahmed said, "Woman, leave me alone! I have a book to read." Ahmed read the Gospel of Luke, the book of the Bible most suited for Muslims, because it speaks of the Samaritan's honor, the prodigal son's dishonor, and other themes of shame and honor.

Ahmed gave himself over to God. Over a period of three months, he was miraculously healed of the paralysis in his left leg! Ahmed plants churches today.

This is the usual start for Muslim evangelization: most often, Muslims are told that either God has a wonderful plan for their lives or that Jesus Christ, the Son of God, died for their sins. But more than anything—more than being assured that they will be saved from their sins—Muslims today need to be delivered from a nearly constant state of feeling defilement or shame. Freedom in Christ from defilement is another way of describing salvation.

Here is a better consideration for evangelization: Tell your listeners the story of Adam and Eve. Tell them that Adam and Eve were created without shame, but then they sinned and had to hide from their shame and defilement. Our Muslim convert church in Paris is led by an Algerian convert who came to Christ by reading the story of Adam and Eve in the garden. That's right! He saw that although Adam and Eve

were defiled, God never left them. God called for them, He clothed them, He corrected them, He gave a promise to them, and He kept them alive.

Muslims have never heard that God "associates with," or dialogues with, and cherishes and even loves defiled people. In fact, the greatest form of blasphemy in Islam is the concept of *"syirik"*—that is, that God associates with and cares for defiled people—because for Muslims, if God were to link Himself to human beings, this would diminish His greatness. As Muslims say, *"Allah-U-Akbar,"* or "God is great," which Muslims also take to mean we are worthless. (God never associates with humans.) But in Christ, Ahmed went from "worthless and defiled" to useful and valuable to Christ.

Questions for the Reader

1. Muslims are more hospitable than we can imagine. Would you ask a Muslim if you could eat at his or her house—today? Respond below.

2. If you asked a Muslim about the challenges he/she faced last week, would you pray for these challenges?

CHAPTER 3

Don't Convert Muslims Twice: Cultural Meddling Turns Conversion into a Double Conversion

Paul uses this knockout concept that shows the radical nature of his evangelism:

For though I am free of all people, I have made myself a slave to all, that I might win the more. And to the Jews I became as a Jew, that I might win Jews; to those who are under the Law, as under the Law, though not being myself under the Law, that I might win those who are under the Law; to those who are without law, as without law, though not being without the law of God but under the law of Christ, that I might win those who are without law. To the weak I became weak, that I might win the weak; I have become all things to all men, that I may by all means save some. And I do all things for the sake of the gospel, that I may become a fellow par-taker of it. (1 Cor. 9:19–23)

This is not just "passion before track record," as discussed in Chapter 2. Paul became fragile, vulnerable, and weak to win the weak. We understand the apostle's empathy here. However, he also became adept at working with legalistic Jews by accepting them along with their bundle of rules and laws.

We can understand why Paul didn't ask these Jews to drop their laws before he proclaimed Christ to them. Nevertheless, can we understand why Paul continued to follow Jewish law—by shaving his head and circumcising Timothy, for example—even though he said that circumcision counts for nothing before God (1 Cor. 7:19)? So are we to become Muslims to win the Muslims? Would Paul have said this? Would you say this?

The problem isn't as complicated as it sounds. Islam is both a religion and a culture. If we accept the challenge, we should consider adopting part of the Muslim culture to win Muslims to Christ.

Islam has rooted itself into cultures across the world. *A brother, who has lived in the Middle East for eighteen years, says Islam is like a giant vacuum cleaner that pulls in cultures, powers, customs, and fears from across the world and then controls all of these.*

Here is an example of "becoming as" a Muslim in order to reach Muslims. From 1998 to 2003, mission-agency executives forbade the distribution of Bibles in Bangladesh for a very particular reason. The printer of the thousands of Bibles in the new Bangladeshi language had printed the Bibles with a green cover. Mission leaders were outraged because, as they said, "The Bible should have a black cover! A green-colored Bible looks like a Koran. This is just compromise. It must be stopped. Don't ship these containers of Bibles."

For five years these "green" Bibles languished in warehouses until the warehouse space was finally needed and the mission's executives reluctantly released them. When the Bibles were finally shipped, thousands of Bangladeshi Muslims said, "It is green; it looks like 'our color.' We want it."

The mission's executives who had wanted "no compromise" had actually been reacting against the Muslim culture and not against the religion of Islam.

Distributing green Bibles is only one example of accommodating to Muslim culture. How about other, more difficult issues? Would you accept a Muslim who wanted to know Jesus as Lord even if he or she came to your church dressed in a jellaba or another kind of robe, or in a veil, a head covering, a burka, or a hijab? Would such a person feel welcomed and thus want to return to church to meet you again?

What if a Muslim came to your church and wanted to kneel as he or she sought Christ? Or what if this Muslim wanted to face toward Mecca in your church after he or she gave his or her life to Jesus Christ? What if this total newcomer brought a Koran to your church? What if he or she thanked God for Jesus Christ by speaking out praise to Allah in Arabic?

Muslims who are open to Christ are sometimes shocked when they see Christians eat pork. Must the Muslim also learn to eat pork and enter into our culture before he or she comes to Christ? Or should we do as Paul said so dramatically and forcefully in Acts 15:29 before the Jerusalem council: "Do not hinder" or "Do not trouble" the Gentiles who are turning to God?

I was with a group of new Muslim converts to Christ. It seemed that I could use their respect for holy books to better teach them from the Bible. Very carefully, I wrapped up my Bible in a piece of fine cloth. As I went before this group of thirty-two North Africans, I opened up the cloth and lifted up the Bible and read from it. You could have heard a pin drop. It didn't cost me much to present a living example of respect for God's Word that these converts could relate to from their own Islamic cultural background.

Many pastors in Paris wonder why Muslims rarely come to Christ in their traditional Western churches. Yet during their church services, no one tells stories or provides meals or hospitality as is done in Muslim culture.

We need to reach Muslims through their own culture. In fact, I propose that we should even *encourage* Muslims to maintain their culture. Shout it from the housetops: *Let Muslims keep their cultural identity as they come to Christ. Otherwise, how will they ever share with other Muslims who are from their own ethnic group or community?*

No Algerian should first become Western before he or she comes to Christ. Cultural conversion is a walling off, a blocking off, of the natural spread of the Gospel through the God-given channels of family, clan, and friendships. When a new baby comes to your family, guess who changes most? The parents change, the parents prepare, the parents make adjustments, and the parents accept the "tender frame" of the newborn.

In 1 Corinthians 7:17–24, Paul insists on small cultural or social changes as the Gentiles converted to Christianity and came into contact with formerly Jewish Christians. Paul's words are painfully direct:

> Only, as the Lord has assigned to each one, as God has called each, in this manner let him walk. And thus I direct in all the churches. Was any man called beforehand as circumcised? Let him not become uncircumcised. Has anyone been called in uncircumcision? Let him not be circumcised. Circumcision is nothing, and uncircumcision is nothing, but what matters is the keeping of the commandments of God.
>
> Let each man remain in that condition in which he was called. Were you called while a slave? Do not worry about it; but if you are also able to become free, rather do that. For he who was called in the Lord while a slave, is the Lord's freedman; likewise he who was called while free, is Christ's slave. You were bought with a price; do not become slaves of men. Brothers, let each man remain with God in that condition in which he was called.

Admittedly, some Muslim cultural norms may be a hindrance to the propagation of the Gospel. The sooner we can bring Muslims into a relationship with Jesus Christ, the sooner the Holy Spirit can bring change that we ourselves can't bring without being paternalistic and culturally dominant toward these sons and daughters of Abraham.

Challenge: My dream is the creation of fellowships of Muslim-background believers who maintain their cultural traditions, their dress, and their way of seeing Christ formed in them and in their culture.

Question: Have you met Muslims who are really seeking God?

Case Study 3
Butros, a Muslim Friend
Whom God Loves

Before his conversion from Islam, Butros was an imam, or Muslim cleric, who built and oversaw mosques in Algeria. He had built twenty-two mosques by acting as a fund raiser and general contractor. He solicited the funds and organized the placement of other imams and the leadership of all twenty-two mosques, whose leaders remained under his tutelage. He was known as a grand imam, one who made Islam flourish. But then God entered the scene. A mysterious person sent

Butros's family a Gospel of Luke. This event blew up the family, causing much anger and rage. Then, just as suddenly, the Gospel of Luke was strangely lost.

The Gospel then turned up when the family sold its home and moved. The Luke portion turned up in the packing boxes, and this, in a word, was the key to Butros's coming to faith in Christ.

Butros joined us in France as part of our Muslim-background believer fellowship. His knowledge of the Bible, of the Koran, and of the Arab language is just beyond belief.

Butros's life has undergone a radical change through his salvation. However, his inner peace hasn't changed his difficult outward circumstances. As is typical when a Muslim converts to Christianity, Butros's Muslim brothers have vowed that he should die.

Butros was also rejected by the French. He diligently worked for six weeks in Paris and afterward was refused any salary payment. This happened twice until finally he became part of a sort of indentured labor force.

He lives with his Muslim aunt in Paris, but she has also turned on him, causing him enormous insults and abuse. For example, she accuses him of being to blame for every difficulty the family has experienced. In fact, in an attempt to control him, she even tries to lock him in the house sometimes! Butros feels this is one of many ways his aunt tries to brainwash him into accepting Islam again.

Butros wants to return to Algeria to help care for his mother, who has Alzheimer's disease. His own two natural brothers, who are both imams, are in Algeria as well. They have vowed to hurt him, or worse. This is because Butros's whole family is part of a radical Islamic branch with a clerical heritage.

Butros's sister (married to a Frenchman) had just traveled back to Algeria to visit the family, whose fervor was transforming into a new level of Islamic radicalism. (Typically, when a Muslim like Butros converts to Christ, the family becomes more virulently Muslim.) Now Butros's sister had returned as an even more determined Islamist as a result of contact with Butros's extremist family: she left France as a secularized Muslim and returned from Algeria as a completely veiled radical.

If you have a heart for Butros and other former Muslims like him who can't find traction in France, please pray for them. And there are more just like Butros, who was saved miraculously by the sale of his parent's home and the discovery of the mysterious Gospel of Luke. We need people like

Butros who are too radical and too outspoken for most established churches, but yet who are gloriously humble in Christ and knowledgeable about the North African mind.

Butros wants to care for his family, to reach the lost, and to pour himself out to Jesus Christ. Do you think that the pull of Islam can change the heart of born-again Butros back to Islam when he visits his family in Algeria? How can we surround brothers like Butros so he can be used of God, protected, cared for, trained, and allowed to flower in his ministry? Pray for Butros.

Questions for the Reader

1. We talk very little about evil spirits. How would you react to a Muslim who has an evil spirit, or jinni? Develop your thoughts below.

2. Can you discuss what brings shame and dishonor to a Muslim?

CHAPTER 4

Shame and Honor

Muslims are part of a shame-and-honor culture, a society vastly different from the Western guilt-and-consequence culture. A Muslim who is shamed is a Muslim who feels defiled. The common motto among Muslims is that death is better than being dishonored.

To preserve their honor, Muslims are particularly concerned with external rites, such as not eating pork, the direction to face while they sleep, and using appropriate greetings. They actively wash their hands and feet before reading the Koran so that external ablutions can wash away defilement. If they have sex outside of marriage, they can regain their lost honor through a ritual bath.

It is important to not confuse shame with guilt—guilt is absent among Muslims. Although their world is turned upside down when they are shamed, Muslims reject guilt entirely. The Turks have a saying, "Even if guilt were made of silk, no one would wear it." Guilt must never be confessed, they say, because it would result in a loss of honor (which, again, is worse than death itself).

Instead, any guilt one feels must be passed on to someone else. Responsibility for evil is attributed to those outside of Islam, whom they call the "House of War," or "*Dar al-Harb*," whereas the "*Dar al-Islam*" ("House of Islam") includes all the faithful. A real-life usage of this term is the predominantly Muslim capital city of Tanzania, which is named Dar es Salaam, another variant of "House of Islam." Islam has indeed divided and polarized the world into those who are Muslims (those who have submitted) and the world of unbelievers, or infidels.

In contrast, the Western guilt-and-consequence culture gives a high value to taking responsibility for sins like lying and cheating. Guilt and consequences are important issues in our jobs, in our spiritual matters of faith, and in our public dealings and businesses.

The stark contrast between the shame/honor and the guilt/consequence cultures has often been a point of difficulty for missionaries. Missionaries to Muslims often feel dismayed that the Muslim culture has no sense of right and wrong. Muslims don't feel they have broken God's law, so how can we bring them to a saving faith if they don't feel guilty?

Hope is not lost! As missionaries or as friends of Muslims, we have two choices about how to bring salvation to Muslims. Our first choice is to cause them to abandon their shame-and-honor culture in exchange for our guilt-and-consequence culture. We can say to the person who has had sex outside of marriage that the washing or ablution is without merit, and that washing one's hands and feet before opening a holy book is unnecessary.

However, discrediting these rituals could possibly weaken the relationship you have with this Muslim, or at worst could result in a secularizing influence in the Muslim's mind-set. Saying "Rituals don't matter" is a Western approach that encourages secularization. As a fellow Christian worker, I would agree that Christian missionaries have a dangerous potential for acting as the greatest secularizing force in the world among Muslims. *Brushing aside Muslim ways of life and describing them as superstitious beliefs can introduce a secular system into their lives.* Do we want this?

Another consequence of denying Muslims their cultural rituals is that we are denying them their world view instead of leading them to Christ within their world view. Without their world view, they are stripped of certain levels of spiritual conscience and are made unable to process new spiritual thoughts. Again, is this what we seek?

The second choice in bringing salvation to Muslims is to not discredit their rituals, but instead to focus on how God knows and understands their shame. It is a fair and even biblical world view to think of sin as dishonor. The Bible addresses the problem of guilt, but it also speaks volumes about dishonor, which Muslims can relate to.

For example, in a ritual to honor God, Aaron and his sons were to wash their hands and feet whenever they entered the tent of meeting or approached the altar; otherwise they would die (Exod. 30:17–21).

We can also read John 4 and the story of the Samaritan woman, who was "defiled" because she had lived with five men. ("Defilement" is a cousin word to "shame," not to "guilt"). Yet Jesus never rejected her, and He even asked to drink from this Samaritan's cup, which was defiled in the eyes of the Jews because her lips had touched it. Jesus understood her defilement and accepted her as she was.

But the even greater implication about defilement that we can take from this story is not just that Jesus understood and accepted the Samaritan woman, but that Jesus also gave her *living* water to receive and thus completely remove her defilement: "Whoever drinks the water I give him will never thirst. Indeed, the water I give him will become in him a spring of water welling up to eternal life" (John 4:14). Jesus is the only answer to defilement and cultural or religious estrangement. With Jesus, you aren't forever a prisoner of your past behavior. Jesus was greater than the defilement of a Samaritan woman's present and past lives.

The Bible is the Word of God for all people. Yet it is essentially an Eastern book. The Bible often deals with shame and honor. Let's take a look at a few more verses in which I've emphasized these themes:

> If anyone is *ashamed* of me and my words, the Son of Man will be *ashamed* of him when he comes in his glory and in the glory of the Father and of the holy angels. (Luke 9:26)
>
> "For both He who sanctifies and those who are sanctified are all from one Father, for which reason He is not ashamed to call them brethren. (Heb. 2:11)
>
> If they shall fall away, to renew them again unto repentance; seeing they crucify to themselves the Son of God afresh, and put him to an open shame. (Heb. 6:6–7)
>
> There is no one righteous, not even one. (Rom. 3:10)

All our righteous acts are like filthy rags. (Isa. 6:46)

You could easily tell a Muslim that he or she must honor God and God's people as well. We can base many good questions on the Muslim sense of honor and defilement; for example, why not ask a Muslim if he or she knows that we human beings are all defiled? Doors swing open through this great starting point.

Description of a Muslim Ritual

According to the Koran (Al-An'am: 6), Allah orders purification from minor impurities by *wudhu* ("ablution") and from major impurities by *ghusl* ("bathing") ahead of *salat* ("prayer"). Here is a description of *wudhu*.

1. Make *niyyaah* (intentions) to remove the state of impurity by performing *wudhu* (ablution).
2. Say "*bismillah*" (In the Name of Allah).
3. Wash the hands three times.
4. Wash the mouth three times. (One must make sure that water reaches all parts of the mouth, all the way to the back.)
5. Rinse the nostrils with water three times. (One needs to be careful when doing this

while fasting, so as not to get water into the throat.)

6. Wash the face three times, upward from the place where the hair of the head grows to the lower part of the chin lengthwise and across from one ear to the other. The beard is a part of the face, which should be washed on the surface, even if it is thick. It is preferable to pass the fingers through it.

7. Wash the hands up to the elbows three times.

8. Wipe all the head, by passing wet hands from the front of the head until they reach the back of the head and then return back to the front again. The ears are to be wiped after the head from the interior to the exterior parts by inserting two index fingers in the two holes of the ears and rotating the thumb on the outer parts.

9. Wash the feet up to the ankles three times. During ablution, all parts of the body to be washed should be submerged in water— that is, letting the water flow over them. If the water does not reach any of these parts, ablution will be invalid. Ibn Umar reported that a man who was performing ablution left a portion equal to the size of

a nail unwashed of his right foot. On sighting him, the Prophet (Salla Allahu Alaihi Wa Sallam) said, "Go back and perform ablution thoroughly."

Challenge: Paul (Rom. 9:33) and Peter quote Isaiah on the subject. "See, I lay a stone in Zion, a chosen and precious cornerstone, and the one who trusts in Him will never be put to shame" (1 Pet. 2:6). I dream of presenting Christ and the Gospel in a way that addresses my defilement and shame as well as my guilt and sin.

Question: Can I, as a Westerner, find a depth in my relationship with God as I consider biblical areas of shame, honor, and defilement, and not just sin and guilt? If Jesus was tempted in every way that we are, was He faced with an understanding of the temptation to defilement and dishonor in every way as Muslims do? He "endured the cross, scorning its *shame*" (Heb. 12:2).

Case Study 4
Muhammad and Djamela, Muslim Friends Whom God Loves

Our way into the home of Muhammad and Djamela began when I told them, "I am going to eat at your house today or very soon." Muhammad was stunned, not because we insisted on eating with them, but because we would want to eat with any Muslim.

He said, "I'm honored. We haven't had a single Frenchman in our home, nor have we eaten with them in their homes."

That night in Muhammad and Djamela's home, we took off our shoes, as is custom, although at this time we didn't know the importance of this small gesture. To Muslims, removing one's shoes in a home symbolizes removing defilement. So when we took off our shoes, we kept defilement from entering their home.

Defilement is so feared that if a woman has her menstrual cycle during Ramadan, the month of fasting, Muslims believe that her prayers are not heard. Muslims consider Christians to be defiled because Muslims associate all manner of pornography and impure living with what they call "Christian countries." So when we took off our shoes, we explained that we are "*hanifi*" Christians—that is, Christians who have the faith of Abraham. Calling ourselves "*hanifi* Christians" seemed to distance ourselves from the defilement of what they think Christians are.

Later, our trainee Ashley, who was with us, recited the story of Adam and Eve to Muhammad and Djamela in Arabic. The story caused a tenderness to God in that household. It only took a little willingness to share the story of the fall in the Garden of Eden, where God was faithful to His people, who were full of shame. When Ashley recited the story of Adam and Eve's fall, she was telling the story of the defilement of the first two human beings on earth.

Islam also teaches the fall of Adam and Eve, but without God calling out, "Adam, where are you?" after Adam is defiled. In the same way, Muslims don't teach that God calls to us today (in our defilement), "Let Me make clothes to cover your nakedness [defilement] and shame." When Ashley recited the story of Adam and Eve, you could have heard a pin drop on those French tiles in Muhammad and Djamela's home. They could hardly believe that even though Adam and Eve were defiled, God did not reject them.

We finished eating with Muhammad and Djamela, and what Muhammad had to say next mystified us. He said he would rescue us, protect us, take care of us, defend us from any attack or from any robbers, or help us fix anything in our house that needed repair. I wondered the reason behind this dramatic promise that he could become our police, midnight plumber, and new caretaker.

Muhammad was engrafting us into a circle of friendship that, in Islam, extends worldwide in the *ummah*, or the "people of the faith." He was offering us more than we had dreamed was possible. (The *ummah* today is not only the people of Islam, but extends to the culture of the Arab Muslim nations.) The only way he could accept us was to say, "I will take care of you, I will defend you, I will be your plumber at the midnight hour." What a privilege it was to first enter into Muhammad and Djamela's *ummah*, even as an honorary member. Honoring them and their honoring us both happened before we could bring them into our own *ummah*, our family of God in Christ Jesus.

Questions for the Reader

1. If a Muslim says that Jesus is a prophet of God, what would be your response? Write it below.

2. How soon would you baptize a formerly Muslim follower of Jesus?

CHAPTER 5

The Fish Scale

The original Engel's Chart shown below, formulated by James Engels, follows the typical journey of conversion to Christ among Western people. The chart shows the roles of God, of the communicator, and of the person's response as he or she becomes more and more aware of the implications of the Gospel.

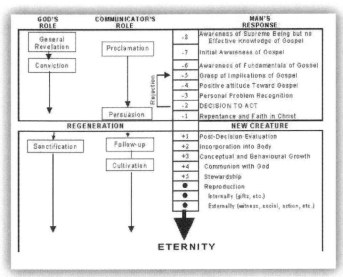

Figure 1. Engel's Chart.

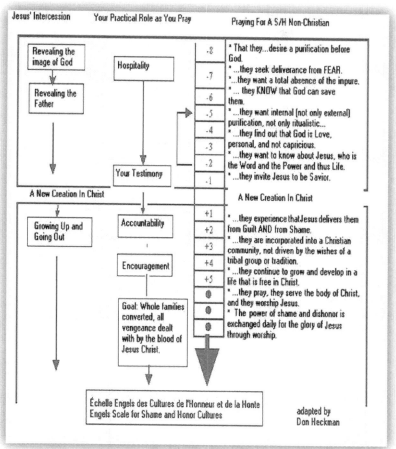

Figure 2. The Modified Engel's Scale for Shame-and-Honor Peoples.

The disadvantage of the Engel's Chart, however, is that it fits the changes that take place inside the Westerner, but relates only marginally to Eastern peoples. Therefore, after studying and interviewing the conversion process of many Muslims, I have put together a new chart that lists the steps that most Muslims go through as they come to Christ as Lord. The chart is called the Fish Scale (a tongue-in-cheek way of using the "fish symbol" of Christianity and the scale of how a person comes to Christ), or, more formally, the Modified Engel's Scale for Shame-and-Honor Peoples.

What is the difference between the Muslim's coming to Christ and a Westerner's coming to Christ? The biggest issue is the difference between the Western guilt-and-consequence culture and the Eastern shame-and-honor culture (see Chapter 4). Muslims live in a world of shame and honor, and not in a traditional Western system of guilt and consequences. (Note: Postmodern Westerners and younger adults in the West are also more concerned with their shame and honor: for example, "cool" and "uncool" relate to corporate honor and shame).

The Bible addresses both world views; *even though the Bible addresses the problem of guilt, it also speaks volumes about honoring.*

Description of the Fish Scale
The Modified Engel's Chart uses a series of numbers from negative eight to five (−8 to +5) to show the process of conversion to Christ among Muslims and other Eastern shame-and-honor peoples. Note

that the large boxes in the chart divide the negative numbers from the positive numbers to emphasize the Muslim convert's need to grow and become a productive and fruitful believer. As God is honored (going from negative eight to five), the defilement and dishonor is also lifted off the Muslim who turns to Christ as Lord. Keep in mind that because we are dealing with people of an "oral culture" (see Chapter 6), much of the chart can be taught to Muslims in an oral, storytelling fashion.

Before going through the chart, I'd like to tell the story of Raashida, a young Muslim Moroccan lady, and Muhammad, a Muslim man, both of whom came to Christ as a result of reviewing this chart. Raashida and Muhammad attended a teaching session at our church on the Modified Engel's Chart. Raashida cried out loud. She said that God was revealing Himself in her life and that she must come to Christ. After the session Muhammad went for a fifteen-mile walk around Paris for hours, crying out to God, and finding Him as Father in his life. Muhammad, an Algerian Muslim once trapped in a Nietzschean philosophy, is attending a Bible school today.

The left column (entitled "Jesus's Intercession") describes the role of Jesus Christ in the Muslim's conversion. A curious and unexpected response occurs as Muslims consider Christ as Lord. As Raashida and Muhammad came closer to Christ, their families became more radicalized in Islam to maintain honor. Prayer is essential here. *A Muslim man or woman in France, for example, often becomes more radicalized in Islam than they were in North Africa as a defense mechanism against the prevailing Western culture.* The Spirit of God literally sustains new converts as they come to Christ against all odds. Yes, the ideal scenario is for the whole family to come to Christ. However, many Muslim married couples come to Christ with the husband giving his life to Christ before the wife will convert. Why? *Because of shame and honor. Muslim wives are not only under the obligation to honor their husbands, but to also honor their own fathers and their families, and to thus remain in Islam for the sake of their entire family's honor.*

The middle column (entitled "Your Practical Role as You Pray") describes your role. Share and receive hospitality with Muslims as you share your testimony in story form. The role of encouragement is crucial in bringing Muslims to Christ because of the vulnerability they feel. Blood vengeance, fears, demonic attacks, and family honor will continue to try to persuade Muslims to remain faithful within Islam.

The right column (entitled "Praying for a Shame-and-Honor Non-Christian") describes the evolution Muslims go through, from negative eight to five, in becoming the persons Christ wants them to be. Note the lessening levels of defilement and shame. The starting point with most Muslims is a *"desire for purification before God." All Muslims desire this.* To start Muslims in the process of evolving to a level five, we need to fulfill our role in showing hospitality (notice the box labeled "Hospitality"). This involves both caring for them as well as praying for their fears. This isn't just theory—we have seen Muslims come to Christ simply through victory over fear and the haunting conviction that they are defiled, thus jumping from a negative seven to a positive number (which signifies that they are a new creation in Christ). Our goal is that they can know that God can save them. Most don't realize this fact of God's love.

Challenge: Viewing God from a shame-and-honor point of view places the concept of holiness outside the realm of just avoiding certain sins. Honoring God moves us from just escaping sin to the bigger issue of bringing God into His rightful honor everywhere and at all times in our lives.

Question: How can a godly honoring of Muslim converts help launch us into their world of an oral communication culture? How can we learn their stories of how God was working in their lives even before they became converted to Christ?

Case Study 5
Rosa, a Muslim Friend
Whom God Loves

Pray for wives and women. Our church in Paris of eighty-five Muslim converts has very few single women who have a Muslim background. Most women are under the *dual authority of their fathers and of their husbands.*

Rosa is one of our church members who struggled with this. Her father was a devout Muslim, but her husband, Mohand, was a Christian who had met the Lord two years earlier. Rosa wanted to become a Christian, so she went to her father to ask for permission. Can you imagine this? If her father said no, she was ready to divorce her husband to maintain her family commitment of being true to Islam.

Rosa, like most Muslim wives, could not make an individual decision without honoring her father and thus honoring her family name. (Group decisions for Christ based on honor for family are very foreign in a Western cultural world view.) Muslim women are literally women of submission, women of Islam. Their lives need prayer because of their often-abusive situations and their fears.

So Rosa asked her Muslim father whether she should become a Christian or whether she should divorce her husband. The father fled the room in a dramatic show of anger, offended that she would even raise this question.

Then a miracle happened. Rosa spent the next three nights at her father's house. During the night she saw a light appear to her, asking her, "Rosa, what do you want me to do for you?" She screamed at the sight of a spirit that spoke like a flashing light. Her mother advised her to simply drink half a glass of water to drive out the evil spirits from her bedroom.

The light appeared a second time and then a third. The third night that this light spoke to her was a defining moment for Rosa. She recognized the kindness of the voice in the light as the Father in heaven whom her husband talked about. As she mused about the light being a revelation of God speaking to her, her husband knocked on the door that third night. He said, "Rosa, please come back to us and to our family." She jumped up and said, "I will follow you, I will be your wife, and the Lord Jesus Christ will be my Lord." Dreams and visions are exceedingly common in the Muslim world.

Years earlier, when Rosa had her first daughter, Fatima, she dedicated her daughter to the *jinni*, or to Satan. I asked why she did this. She thought that a child dedicated to Satan would be free from satanic attacks in life. Fatima's dedication to Satan had been for her protection.

Questions for the Reader

1. Miriam says that she practices the jihad. What does she mean? Write your answer below.

2. Would you allow a Muslim convert to attend your church if he wears his robe? If he prays to Jesus facing Mecca? If he removes his shoes and prays on the carpet, face down?

CHAPTER 6

Become a Storyteller

Ninety percent of the unreached world consists of **oral peoples**, for whom the nature of communication is telling stories. For these people, storytelling is not only the way they communicate but also the most effective way to spread the Gospel. Oral peoples can usually recite back 80 percent or more of your story. In comparison, Western people can usually recite back 25 percent or less of your story.

Muslims belong to this oral population, whether they are literate or illiterate. I've told stories to Muslim converts in Kabylia, Tamanrasset, and Algiers, Algeria, and elsewhere in Africa. After two years, they could recite the stories to me almost word for word. Like a photograph, each story told is a story remembered. A story remembered is a story that they can retell to others within their culture, their home, and their town.

This is good news, and not just because Muslims can remember a story word for word. They simply love to listen to stories—even if it's a Bible story! They love Bible stories because the Koran mentions biblical stories but without much detail. Here are some of the Bible stories Muslims enjoy:

Adam and Eve	Abraham	The Fall in Eden
Jacob and Esau	Jesus and Lazarus	Moses and Aaron
The Birth of Jesus	Job and David	The Good Samaritan
Mary	The Prodigal Son	

My, Your Story

Let's think of the future, too. How will a Muslim convert communicate the Gospel to his or her clan or people? Nothing is more important than repeating an oral tradition as the (Bible story) tradition or (your) story. Stories become part of their very culture in Christ for future generations. Also, Muslim children who learn stories from you can convey them to their parents and extended families. Oral communication, namely storytelling, is the key to reaching Muslims.

How to Tell Stories to Muslims

The key to storytelling is that the story is recited, never read. Tell them the story of God's Word not by reading a story, but by retelling it to them (see the section "Use Interactive Learning" in Chapter 8). I made the mistake of not telling the story recently.

I gave a Gospel to Asamaa, a twenty-year-old Moroccan woman, but instead of telling the story, I circled the page number in the Bible. For Muslims, writing in the Bible, like in the Koran, is considered a defiling of a holy book. Oops! More on this on page 70.

Another key to telling stories is to avoid using the Western format we are subconsciously programmed to use. For example, Westerners often think of using outlines as a professional, well-prepared, and thought-out form of communication. However, oral people may find using outlines to be cold and distant. Here are some more noted differences between communicating the Gospel in a Western format and communicating the Gospel among Muslims and oral peoples:

Ways of communicating the Gospel in a Western format

- Using outlines
- Teaching with lists
- Emphasizing individual, not group, obedience
- Emphasizing logic
- Preaching
- Confronting the listener

Ways of communicating the Gospel among Muslims and oral peoples

- Using examples
- Telling a story and having your audience retell it
- Encouraging memorization
- Using parables
- Tying real life to particular story events
- Citing proverbs

The Bible Is the Ultimate Guide to Storytelling
The Bible itself teaches us through stories: no less than 75 percent of the biblical text is "storytelling," or oral communication. The Old Testament is full of life stories dealing with God's action, His people's response, His love, and His heart. The New Testament tells the stories of the woman who lost the coin, Thomas's doubt when Jesus appeared to him, the two women who paid for Jesus's expenses, the healing of the paralytic, and many others. Even the genealogies of Matthew contain the stories of God's dealings in the lives of His people.

Study the invaluable methods of Jesus. Jesus used parables to communicate with the Jews, who were also an oral people. The Parable of the Sower allows the listener to place himself or herself as an active participant in the story. No parable can demonstrate the Gospel's call for us to be freed from religion as forcefully as the Parable of the Good Samaritan. Each story is a mirror of the heart, a Gospel message to be retold to others, and a radical call to discipleship.

Also, study the methods of other Bible characters. David, for example, noted the importance of always being ready to communicate stories. Furthermore, Psalms 45:1 says, "My heart overflows with a goodly theme; I address my verses to the king; my tongue is like the pen of a ready writer." So what does this verse mean? My tongue is always ready to communicate my heart and the heart of God my King, whether through stories, laments, or songs.

Your Stories Reflect Your Self

To Muslims, stories and oral communication are a reflection of a person's heart. Muslims say that the first things that a person says are the most important issues of that person's life. This is why Muslims will speak of God, of Allah, almost immediately. Westerners are cautioned in the West to be discreet and hesitant in sharing their faith, which is mostly a private faith. This is not the case with oral, Eastern peoples.

Oral communication with Muslims is a public event, just as Muslims communicate their shame and honor publicly. If you avoid communicating what is on your heart to Muslims because you want to find an opportune time for your thoughts, Muslims may interpret that to mean that you're hiding something. They'll trust you more if you share Jesus without hesitation or without waiting for that "magic moment."

What a gift this understanding is to missionaries! Muslims are already effectively making us, as Christian workers, more and more radical. They are transforming our discreet "Western" sharing into a more integrated lifestyle of speaking the Word and Life into an oral, Eastern context. *Oral communications with Muslims will radicalize you.*

Challenge: The most powerful example of public, oral communication is the *ummah*. Muslims are part of this *ummah*, the underground railroad of a "global Islamic community allegiance." Muslims in London feel welded to, or even like a cloned part of, the community of oppressed fellow Muslims in Palestine, for example. A rumor that the Koran was dishonored in one country caused a riot in Pakistan, an entirely different country.

Question: Can we use this "underground railroad" for Christ instead, to create a oneness in

Christ among former Muslims who are converted to Christ?

Case Study 6
Chafic and Suade, Muslim Friends Whom God Loves

Chafic and his wife, Suade, came to our home. We sat down for a while as we greeted them. Suade wore her head covering. Then I brought out a bilingual New Testament in Arabic and in French. I turned to the Parable of the Prodigal Son in Luke 15 so they could follow the story as I described it to them.

Suade had previously met our trainee, Ashley, in the open vegetable market when Ashley spoke a few Arabic words to a vendor. Suade said, "Come to my home now; it is urgent. You must follow me." Dressed in a black covering that covered her from head to foot, Suade seemed hospitable yet imposing. My wife, Evey, went with Ashley to visit Suade, who pronounced the blessing of God as she entered her apartment. Suade later brought her husband, Chafic, along to our home.

As we began telling the prodigal son story from Luke 15, something amazing happened. Chafic took over and started to read the story himself. Then he became animated and began commenting on the story: "He insulted his father! He came back defiled, but his father ran to see him? Why did his father do that?" I lost my job of telling the story. I could see God at work in Chafic. The secret was to turn Chafic's hunger over to God, rather than to make myself too much of an answer man. My Muslim friend showed that the Spirit of God was at work in his life. Clearly, he had been seized by the living Word!

Later, Chafic invited us over to his home for couscous, a traditional Moroccan meal. Hospitality was Chafic's honorable way of saying that God was speaking to him and that he wanted to know more about God in the context of a meal together. God spoke. Hospitality was the response.

Now, Suade is a woman of Islamic power. After pronouncing a blessing at her apartment door when Ashley and Evey visited her, she told the ladies how breastfeeding her nephew made him her son, according to Islam. (In Islam, after a mother breastfeeds a child five times, that child becomes her child for nearly every practical purpose. Now she has one more mouth to feed.) She was ensconced in traditions like following the required Islam-approved side of the body to sleep on at night, special Islamic greetings, a particular way to blow her nose, and which foot to use first upon entering a bathroom.

How did the reading of the story of the prodigal son speak to the heart of a ritualistic, fundamentalist Islamic couple like Suade and Chafic? The story became not only a lesson on dishonor and acceptance but so much more. Symbolic or charismatic and highly ritualized Muslims like Suade and Chafic are missing one thing, and that's love and acceptance in a very cold and fearful world of punishment and judgment. They translated the prodigal's father as a keyhole into an unknown life outside of the pain and sorrow of darkness. It wasn't hard to see them equate us with the prodigal's father. That father didn't fit their categories, nor did we. We reflected the care shown by the prodigal's father, a strange but real alternative in God to their constant magical and ritualistic sayings, like "*Bismallah*," which means "in the name of God"; "*Inshallah*," which means "if God so wills"; "*Du'a*" before entering the toilet area; or "*Dhikr*" when the evil whisper of Satan comes upon them. Our response was John 4:18: "There is no fear in love, but perfect love casts out fear. For fear has to do with punishment, and he who fears is not perfected in love." Suade is not yet a Christian, but she is very committed to Ashley and to Evey. She needs to know the strength of a Christian community.

Questions for the Reader

1. What hospitality gift can you give a Muslim whom you are visiting? Note your answer below.

2. A Muslim who becomes a follower of Christ is often rejected by his or her family. This convert now hates other Muslims just as he or she hates Islam; he or she wants only the Bible and Jesus, nothing else. What would you say to this person?

CHAPTER 7

Define Your Terms

Define your terms to Muslims, because they are confused by myths and theories about Christians, just as we have misconceptions of what they believe. We can also agree with many terms Muslims use. For example, when Muslims say that Jesus wasn't crucified by men, we can say that they are partially correct—Jesus was the master of His fate, so He permitted His crucifixion to happen. In John 10:18, Jesus says, "No one takes it [my life] from me, but I lay it down of my own accord. I have power to lay it down, and I have power to take it again; this charge I have received from my Father." The point is, we can avoid much unnecessary confrontation if we are careful with our words.

Let's consider the example of Paul. Paul's method was to use terms that non-Christians understood rather than using Christianized terms. In other words, he contextualized terms. Below are a few examples:

- Paul did not offend people with terms and concepts they would not understand (Acts 13:16–24).
- Paul affirmed the Greeks in their religiousness (Acts 17:22).
- Paul affirmed that cultures and peoples will find Jesus in their culture (Acts 17:26, 27).
- Paul did not condemn the Greeks with their polytheism (Acts 17:23).
- Paul quoted nonbiblical literature, quoting Epimenides (Titus 1:12), who described Zeus as God. In the same way, we can affirm a small part of the Koran if it helps Muslims understand "Isa al-Masih"—that is, that Jesus is the Messiah. The Koran is a point of credibility for certain people. Our first approach should never be to reject the Koran openly.
- Paul used foreign language and respected foreign culture (Acts 16:1–5).
- Paul gave people the benefit of considering them as "God seekers" or "God fearers" (Acts 6:9, 13:16).

If we follow Paul's example and use definitions similar to those of our Muslim friends, we will find significant points of similarity between ourselves and them. Then we can use these points of similarity to lead Muslims into conversations where biblical perspectives can enter their world view. Here are a few of those key terms that we can contextualize so Muslims can accept them.

The Gospels

The Gospels, or the New Testament, are known among Arab speakers as the "Injil." Some Muslims honor the Injil, while others feel that it was corrupted by unscrupulous disciples of Christ. But the Koran itself points out the value of the Injil: "In truth He has sent down to you the Book" (thus validating the Torah), and "...the Injil previously sent to you; which are guidance for people. Those that do not believe in the miracles of Allah, they will be severely punished: Allah is Omnipotent and he is the Avenger" (Koran 3:3–4).

Muslims can be told to be confident in the Gospels because the disciples of Christ had no motive to alter the Gospels. Why? Because Muslims and the Koran were not even in existence until the seventh century AD, long after the New Testament was written. The issue here is not primarily whether Muslims feel the New Testament was changed. (Most Muslims are not aware of this concern.) Most have not seen, read, or heard the stories of the New Testament. Overwhelmingly, Muslims are open to the stories of the New Testament. For the first three hundred years after Muhammad's death, nobody shared the Word of God with Muslims. Our sorrow is that fear, cultural superiority, and isolationism moved Christians to often ignore the value of giving the Word to Muslims. However, better than arguing with Muslims is the simple use of telling the stories of God's Word.

The Trinity

We love the fact that Muslims insist that there is one God, not three. Christians believe in one God as well. Our way of describing the Trinity to Muslims is this: first, there is one God. Second, Jesus is known among Muslims as Isa al-Masih (Jesus the Messiah), or the Word of God. Third, the Holy Spirit is the power of God. The Father is the nature of God who gives life, cares for and sustains, and helps mature and protect His people. (When Jesus called God "Father," He wasn't calling on a particular God, but describing one of the aspects or nature of God). We thus avoid portraying our God as three separate gods. Muslims accept this.

The Son of God

Jesus is known among Christians as the "Son of God," a term that is abhorrent to Muslims, because it implies to a Muslim that God had sex with a human. There is no need to avoid the issue of Jesus the Son of God. Sadly, many Christians believe that Jesus's Sonship is due to his birth from Mary. However, no, Jesus existed as Son of God before Mary; he has existed for all eternity, as noted in Psalm 2:7–8: "I will tell of the decree of the LORD: He said to me, 'You are my Son, today I have begotten you. Ask of me, and I will make the nations your heritage, and the ends of the earth your possession.'"

"Son of God" is not a term that describes a little or boyish god or a god who was born; instead, it is a title that signifies Jesus's identical nature with the living God. In Hebrew, "son of" often means "exact nature and personification of." For example, a "son of wickedness" was a wicked person, a "son of strength" was a warrior, and a "son of a bow" was an arrow. In Greek, "son of" has the same meaning. In Mark 3:16–17, Jesus gives James and John the title "sons of thunder" to show that their personality, life, and character were of a thunderous demeanor. In Acts 4:36, Joseph is called "son of encouragement." Nothing here is birth related.

Muslims should know the meaning of "son of" better than we do; Arabic is similar to Hebrew in this sense. For example, Arabic speakers use the term "*ibn-a-heera*," or "son of evil," for an evil person. So if we explain "Son of God" in these terms, Arabic-speaking Muslims will be able to relate. I intentionally push the point that Jesus is the Son of God to open up discussion. "Son of God" is a title of absolute likeness: "If you have seen the Son, you have seen the Father" (John 14:9).

Jesus

If Muslims say that Jesus was a prophet, what should we say? I agree with them. He was a prophet, a priest, a king, the door, the way, the life, the bread, the son, the prince, our peace, and much more. Abraham knew God as Adonai and only later as El-Shaddai. God is Adonai, El-Shaddai, and much more. Abraham knew the full revelation of God only on a progressive basis. If a Muslim tells me that Jesus is the Word, he or she is right. And yet He is more. He is the living God.

The Will of Allah

Before discussing the will of God, we need to talk about Allah. We will need to overcome our Western tendency to say that Allah is not the true God. Our own revelation is progressive; in it we are called to know Him as He really is, more and more. An example of our own partial understanding of God is found in 1 Corinthians 13:12: "For now we see in a mirror dimly, but then face to face. Now I know in part; then I shall understand fully, even as I have been fully understood."

The will of God for Christians is a call to know Him more intimately, with more details of what God wants us to do to serve Him. The will of God for Muslims, in contrast, is a call to remain distanced from God and to accept an obscure fate. Rather than a call to closeness, the will of God for Muslims is a statement of God's unyielding, distant master blueprint. Few Muslims are convinced that God is knowable in an intimate fashion. In fact, even to associate with God is a form of blasphemy within Islam called *"shyrik."*

Storytelling is once again our key to teaching the will of God to a Muslim. Tell Muslims how God was involved in the raising of Lazarus from the dead. Tell how God kept you from danger, or how He encouraged you in the midst of a major setback or in a traumatic accident. Tell how you came to know Him; tell how God sent quail to feed the children of Israel. Tell how God parted the Red Sea and rescued His people from the attack of the armies of Pharaoh. Tell Muslims how you pray to find out God's will. And tell how King David delighted to do the will of God: "Then I said, 'Lo, I come; in the roll of the book it is written of me; I delight to do thy will, O my God; thy law is within my heart'" (Ps. 40:7–8).

Conclusion

Choose your battles. Differences on term definitions are not worth losing your friendship with a Muslim over. And not only are we to choose our battles, but we are also to remain friends with Muslims whether they agree, whether they convert to Christ, or whether they never open their hearts to the Lord in a significant way. Be known as a friend of Muslims whether they come to Christ or not. Pray with Muslims for their healing before they come to Christ. Teach them the Bible even before they come to Christ. You will never know the impact that preconversion discipleship will have on their wider circle of Muslim friends.

Challenge: Even though "discipleship" is sometimes a term for "teaching Christians," it is often referred to as the process of "coming to Christ."

Question: Do we care whether converted Muslims or converted Jews call themselves Christians, Messianic Jews, Members of the Way, or Messianic Muslims? Which term challenges you the most?

Case Study 7
Fatima, a Muslim Friend
Whom God Loves

Fatima, one of our church members, was once destined to become an Islamic marabout, that is, a sorceress or witch doctor. Fatima's sorceress aunt had no daughters, so the dynasty or heritage of the marabout went to Fatima. Just as finances are commonly transferred to a person through an estate or will, Fatima's aunt's power was transferred to Fatima. And so she received the empowerment to foretell the future.

At a church picnic, I asked Fatima how foretelling the future worked. She said that Satan and his demonic hosts told her of their evil plans. If Fatima would not speak about the plans of darkness, she would receive physical wounds and blows from demons. Fatima would have bruises and welts on her face and arms from demons that physically caused her harm in order to intimidate her into speaking about their plans in detail.

Fatima finally broke away from all this after being thrown out of her home by an angry husband. Divorce in Algeria means no support, no income, societal shame, and complete rejection by one's parents. So she was doomed to live like the modern-day leper.

However, God had plans for her. She ran to the Catholic White Fathers, a devout Catholic order in Algeria. The White Fathers had been forbidden from sharing Jesus with Muslims. (The Catholic order has since been shut down by fundamentalists.) One White Father saw Fatima's tears and her heart for God. The priest pointed Fatima toward a newly formed Kabyle church group in Kabylia, an affiliate of our church in Paris. Fatima gave her life to Jesus Christ forever. However, a year later, fanatic religious terrorists in Algeria assassinated that very priest who had showed her the way toward Christ.

Fatima is now teaching on the radio in France, where she broadcasts into Algeria. She is also translating the Bible—both New and Old Testaments—into Kabyle, an Algerian Berber language. There is currently no Kabyle Old Testament, and her work with other scholars and translators is helping to redo the New Testament.

Fatima's latest e-mail to me was in English. Fatima uses "ye" instead of "you" when writing in English, due to the fact that she memorized large portions of the King James English Bible. Fatima, although stone-broke, has become a key contact for church- and mission-based work in Algeria.

Questions for the Reader

1. Some people encourage us to disciple a Muslim before he or she comes to Jesus. What do you think? Write your thoughts below.

2. Women are beaten often by their Muslim husbands. Some have even been victims of acid attacks. How would you restore their destroyed self-worth? How can the Holy Spirit help restore them?

CHAPTER 8

Part I. Muslim Fears and Prayer for God's Compassion

Jesus looked at the people and saw that they were like sheep without a shepherd. Similarly, our hearts are moved with tender compassion when we realize that Muslims live in a world of insecurity, without the certitude of heaven or salvation.

We need to have compassion for the chaos within Islam. The concept of the *"fitra"* among Muslims is the quest for harmony in a world of chaos. *Fitra* is the harmony produced when all things physical submit to what is spiritual. Yet disorder reigns for Muslims.

Fear reigns as well within Islam. Islam is a picture of life without Christ. Consider these verses from the Koran (the numbers at the end of each quote show the sura [chapter] and verse of the Koran):

Allah created first death and then life. (67:2)
Obey Allah only as far as you can. (64:16)
I have done wrong, but my nature is good. (4:28)
People change themselves by their own effort. (13:11)
Muhammad is greater than Moses and Jesus. (33:40)
Jinn [demons] were created to serve Allah. (51:56)
Muhammad gives a message to mankind and to the jinn. (7:38)
When you kill, it isn't done by you, but by Allah. (8:17)
Quitting Islam is the unforgivable sin of betrayal and treachery. (8:27, 71)

Note that most non-Arabic translations of the Koran attempt to soften the harshness of the words of the Koran in order to mask the severity of many statements. A. J. Arberry's is the best Koran translation. It doesn't soften the words of the Koran, and it is probably the best and clearest English translation.

When you share with Muslims, alert your intercessors. You and your team should have intercessors not only for your protection, but also for freedom to walk in the Spirit as you share the Lord Jesus Christ. Pray that God would break our own hearts with compassion. We need to drink from the fountain of compassion and to be freed from anger, bitterness, and revenge.

The Enemy's plan is to harden our hearts against Muslims so we won't care for them. Pray that the Lord humbles us so that our hearts are not superior. Pray that the Lord gives you a sense of a Muslim's point of openness, remembering that our goal is not a quick "confession that Jesus is God." Pray for the courage to invest time and hospitality to care for and love Muslims. Pray for the goal of training Muslim converts, leaders, and teams to continue the work of the expansion of the kingdom of God. Pray that God will keep us from damaging our witness with sinful actions or even the appearance of a compromising situation that would not honor God.

Challenge: What stopped some of the Jews from sharing God's light and the Gospel in the strange culture and strange land of Babylon (see Ps. 137:4)? They preferred their own culture and the city of Jerusalem. The Jews' captors in Babylon asked to listen to the Jews worship the Lord. The Jews refused to witness in a strange culture.

Question: Can prayer soften our hearts so that we can leave the security of our own culture and proclaim Jesus as Lord in a strange culture among Muslims?

Part II. Doors Swinging Open in Islam

Through the Lord's faithfulness, He has left keys to the hearts of all people. Muslims have causeways and paths that lead to their hearts, too. Here are a few tips to opening doors that we have discovered, although there are many more that you will discover as you find your own niche that will help you evangelize among Muslims.

Distinguish Yourself

We should distinguish ourselves as followers of the "God of Abraham." God revealed Himself to Abraham, who "believed God, and it was counted to him as righteousness, and he was called the friend of God" (Jam. 2:23).

Associating Christianity with Abraham is key because Muslims call themselves sons of Abraham. Our experience shows us that we need to identify ourselves with Abraham if we want a fair hearing among Muslims. Furthermore, a faith in the God of Abraham shows that we are aware of the roots of Ishmael, whom they consider as the father of Arab nations.

We should also distinguish ourselves as *"hanufa"* or *"hanifi"* Christians. If we say we are Christians as we share with Muslims, the door to their hearts is often closed. A Christian, to most Muslims, is an immoral, godless Western person. Don't say you are not a Christian. Tell them that you are a *hanufa* or *hanifi* Christian. *"Hanifi"* is used in the Koran strictly to refer to people with the faith or faithfulness of Abraham.

Two Christian Syrian students had never shared with a Muslim even though they were both from a Muslim culture. I encouraged them to share with Muslims by calling themselves *hanufa*. They came back with cries of joy for the way a Muslim man opened his heart to them. It was a first for them.

Use a Muslim World View

Never criticize Muhammad or the Koran. Rarely do arguments or so-called apologetics produce fruit. Instead, ask Muslims what specific verses of the Koran mean. As they share the meaning of selected verses from the Koran, you become a listener and they become storytellers. Try asking them about these somewhat positive verses from the Koran. (Each book of the Koran is called a sura.)

- There are fallen angels, the chief of whom is Satan (Iblis). Satan refused to fall prostrate before Adam. (Sura 7:11, 12)
- Allah created Jesus in the likeness of Adam. (Sura 3:59)
- Jesus performed miracles by Allah's permission. (Sura 5:110)
- God revealed His will through the prophets and apostles. (Matt. 2:15; Sura 16:36)
- All creation has the privilege and duty to worship God. (Ps. 66:4; Sura 1:4)
- "And in their footsteps we sent Isa [Jesus] the son of Mary...we sent him the Injil [the Gospel]: therein was guidance and light, and confirmation of the Tawrah [Old Testament books]." (Sura 5:46)
- **"If you were in doubt as to what we have revealed to you, then ask those [Christians, that is, us] who have been reading the Book [the Bible] from before you." (Sura 10:94)**

Use Interactive Learning

It is very effective to give a Muslim a Bible or a New Testament and have him or her read a Bible story back to you (if he or she is literate). You should have the Muslim read the story in his or her mother tongue, which will probably be Arabic.

Why have Muslims read to you instead of you reading to them? The answer is that the best way for an oral culture person to receive the Word is to physically hear the words of the story. Two things result from "telling back" the story to us. First, the story is reinforced as it is told from the heart. Second, the Muslim can retell the story to other Muslims in an oral fashion.

Here in France, we have found it effective to start the process by giving the Muslim a copy of Luke 15, which tells the story of the prodigal son. As the Muslim reads the story out loud in Arabic, he or she often becomes very animated. The Muslim then tends to erupt in his or her second language, French, and retell us the story in French with amazing excitement.

And why do we use the story of the prodigal son? Many Muslims come to Christ by hearing or reading the prodigal son because it is a story of the father's love that overcomes the dishonor of the son. Moreover, the father's son was defiled by eating with pigs, by living with Gentiles, and by entertaining riotous and depraved friends. The defiled son was openly embraced by a father who dressed him as a person of honor. Muslims see God in this parable. They also see themselves as defiled and dishonored in Islam. Plus, they see hope and love in a way that is never known or dreamed of in Islam.

As they read the story, or as children tell the story to their parents, there will be an eruption of excitement over the events of the story. A public telling of stories seems to open their hearts.

Challenge: Muslims have seen visions of Jesus. However, they don't always understand their revelations. They have heard of Jesus, but they don't know that Isa al-Masih, Jesus Christ, the light of God, is their mediator with God. Visions show that God is at work among Muslims before we arrive.

Question: If the prodigal son story is the story of "defilement and dishonor surmounted," can we show Muslims that Jesus, as the father figure in the prodigal story, can fight against our darkness in a way that ritual purifications never can?

Case Study 8
Ahmed, a Muslim Friend
Whom God Loves

Two recent Muslim converts, Ahmed and Kamina, came to our fellowship, fell in love, and got married. Ahmed decided to lock his new bride, Kamina, into her bedroom every morning for the first three months of their marriage. His Muslim control tendencies lived on.

Ahmed's control of Kamina's life was also hiding his own life of immorality. During the early months of his marriage with Kamina, he was not faithful; he had lady friends from Paris to Algiers. How could a convert to Christ choose to continue in this sin—especially because all throughout his life as a Muslim, Ahmed was taught that defilement could drown his life in darkness?

The reason is that throughout Ahmed's life, he was also taught that immoral lifestyles didn't matter; he only had to take a ritual purification bath to free himself of defilement within Islam. However, if he didn't wash himself after having sex, he would be cursed, and the ground he walked on would also be cursed. Without his Islamic ritual bath, he would be trapped into a state of ritual uncleanness that was more dreaded and appalling than committing adultery.

We taught Ahmed that taking a ritualistic bath would not wash away his defilement. This was a source of great distress to Ahmed, who then began to believe he was trapped in uncleanness. As a Christian, he was no longer able to simply take a ritual bath to wash away his defilement.

Our hardest task was to show Ahmed that his new bath in Christ was his hope to be free from the darkness that pulls us away from our Christian life. Ahmed knew the Islamic way. He never became primarily concerned with sin and guilt. Muslim converts never do so: they are still people who emphasize shame, honor, and defilement even after coming to Christ. So what Ahmed needed was to know that Christ could free him from defilement on a daily basis so that he could experience the close communion with Christ, who alone could direct Ahmed's life.

After we spoke at length with Ahmed about his treatment of Kamina, he still locked her in the house when he left, although now he gave her free reign inside the house. We met again, and only after discussing the issue a third time did Ahmed allow Kamina one bus trip per day. Today Ahmed and Kamina have the trust to love each other without the force of locked rooms. Remember that Ahmed is a servant of Jesus Christ. However, as is often the case with any new convert, many cultural forms and attitudes need to be transformed or rejected.

God's Word applies to the life of a shame-and-honor Christian who gets stuck in the darkness of defilement. Hebrews 12:2 says, "Look to Jesus, the pioneer and perfecter of our faith, who for the joy that was set before Him endured the cross, despising the shame, and is seated at the right hand of the throne of God." Ahmed has to look to Jesus even now, for only Jesus can conquer our shame and defilement. And Jesus's promise to Ahmed, which he is now walking in, is this: "The one who trusts in Him will never be put to shame" (Rom. 9:33). Ahmed is calling upon God to pray into the promise of God's Word of deliverance from shame and defilement.

In Arabic: "Jesus is the Son of God!"

CHAPTER 9

The Mighty Obedience Factor
Can Save Your Life

By modeling and by coaching an insider, you should first change your own prayer group or life group, and then change your outreach to Muslim groups.

Ask these questions, first of yourself, then of one another in your prayer group, and finally to Muslims who read a story that Jesus told:

- What has gone well lately that gave you joy?
- What has caused you, or someone you know, stress lately?
- How did the efforts to help with the stressor we learned the last time go?
- [Have a passage read twice or told twice. Have someone retell the passage. Ask others to fill in any significant details that were omitted when the passage was retold.]

- What do you learn about God from this passage?
- What do you learn about humanity from this passage?
- What would obedience to this passage look like in our lives?
- Who do you know who needs to hear what we have learned today?
- Which of the stressful things that were mentioned earlier can we help to overcome?

Through answering these questions, you and your group will discover something about God's nature and work. You will discover that you can help one another with stressful situations. You will discover the value of being thankful. You will discover the benefits that come from hearing, understanding, and practicing God's Word as a group. You will discover how obedience to a passage is transformational. You discover how to minster to others. And finally, you will discover the importance of sharing what you are learning with others. This works wonderfully with Muslim groups.

In some Christian ministries, we assess how mature a believer is based on how much he or she knows. However, the New Testament assesses the maturity of a believer based on how much he or she obeys. It may not make sense, but a longtime believer can have a high disobedience factor.

Matthew 10:8: "Freely You Received, Freely Give"

- Too often, our current understanding of the word "disciple" or the phrase "being discipled" connotes an idea of receiving, not giving. Jesus taught His followers to pass on all they received.
- Teaching conveys the idea of transferring knowledge, but disciple-making movements convey the idea of changing behavior.

1 Thessalonians 5:17: "Pray without Ceasing"

- God is enthroned on the praises of your heart.
- If you praise Him, as the Bible says, give thanks for everything.
- "…Always giving thanks to the Father for everything, in the name of the Lord Jesus Christ" (Eph. 5:20).
- Give thanks to God also for bad things (Ps. 22:3).
- According to Kevin Greeson, "Men of peace do not descend from heaven, but rise up from Hell."

- If you don't see a disciple's potential via prayer and speak to that person about it, who will?

2 Kings 5

- Why did Elisha allow Naaman take two mules of dirt from
- Israel back to Syria as a talisman?
- Why did the spies go to the house of Rahab, the prostitute?
- Why did God honor Moses, who lied about his wife twice?
- Why did God save Noah, the drunk?
- Why did God protect Cain, the killer of Abel?
- Why did God allow Saul call Samuel back from the dead?
- What was the sin of Balaam, who refused to go with the evil kings?

Obedience stories that Muslims crave in their own lives are as follows:

- Economic trouble: Elijah fed by ravens, 1 Kings 17:1–6
- Sickness: Naaman's healing, 2 Kings 5

- Relationships: lost son, Luke 15:11–32
- Need of hope: water from the rock, Exod. 17:1–7
- Fear: Daniel in the lion's den, Dan. 6:1–28
- Death: rich man and Lazarus, Luke 16:19–31
- Troubling dreams: Nebuchadnezzar, Dan. 4:1–34
- Justice and equality: bricks without straw, Exod. 5:6–18
- Need for peace: Jesus comforts the disciples, John 16:17–33
- Fear of the jinn: Simon the magician, Acts 8:9–25
- Fear of persecution: John and Peter in prison, Acts 4:1–13
- Paranoia and conspiracy: Daniel and the furnace, Dan. 3:1–30

This is your church or your world view: either the top box or the bottom blob. The top box defines followers of Christ as adherents of certain sacred rites, with drunks and evil people outside the box, with no place in your view of the church or you world view. The problem here is that Jesus spent most time with those outside the box, and we use the box often as a fortress defining our beliefs and rejecting the outsiders.

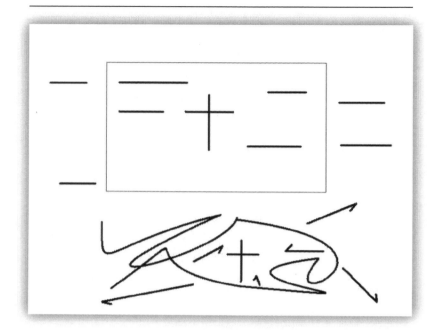

The lower world view is the only way Muslims will come to Christ. Some Muslims are full of witchcraft; adhere to the Koran; practice the jihad; beat their wives; and consider Christians as fallen, outsiders, and worthy of hell, not heaven. The arrows show that some Muslims (or Christians) hold wildly non-Christian beliefs but are moving toward Christ in their love for God. The vector arrows show a better picture of moving toward Jesus. The first picture above describes a state of mind that is rife with satisfied and yet disobedient Christians (although not all Christians in the picture are like this). But what is better, a person who is a seeker of Christ in obedience or a person who thinks he or she has achieved his or her place in Christ but who never knew Him, as in Matthew 7? The weakness of the second picture is that it implies that the kingdom of God includes a lot of flagrant sinners. And truth has never been better spoken.

Questions for the Reader

1. How can you serve a Muslim family?

2. Many converted Muslims still carry talismans and charms for protection. How can you find out if they depend upon charms and spirits for protection?

CHAPTER 10

Doors of Resistance in Islam

1. Ishmael. We have to first look at our own biblical thinking. We call Muslims "cousins" often because they also came from Abraham. However, here is the rub. Some people teach that there was a curse on Ishmael because Abraham "forced" the promise of having a son in his old age by taking Hagar as his concubine, and the true promise came through Isaac. This would mean that Ishmaelites became Muslims because of Abraham's disobedience. Such prejudice hinders our work among Muslims because it casts Muslims in the light of disobedience and of God's rejection.

In actual fact, Ishmael was circumcised (meaning he became part of the covenant) before Isaac was circumcised (Gen. 17:26). God promised that Ishmael would be the father of a great nation of princes (Gen. 17:20); the Ishmaelite traders rescued Joseph from the pit of death (Gen. 37:25); and Joseph brought grain and God's glory to starving Egyptians. The offspring of the Ishmaelites were Arabs, many of whom were praising God at Pentecost (Acts 2:11). Islam stole many Arabs, beginning in the seventh century, away from their call in God.

Islam is not God's punishment for Arabs, but a hijacking of the some of the Arab peoples.

Our work with Arab Muslims is to see God delivers Ishmaelites into their promise of being a great people and a great nation. With this understanding of God's promise about His people, we have overcome one more layer of resistance to reaching Muslims for Christ.

2. Culture. Even though some Christian workers have tried to "save Muslims from their culture," these workers have often succeeded in halting the spread of the Word of God within that culture. Cut the new Muslim believer off from his or her culture and you have set up resistance to ever reaching his or her family.

But how did Jesus deal with the Jewish culture? He used, rejected, and transformed the Jewish culture at different times. How did he do this?

Luke 2:42: At twelve years of age, Jesus attended the temple: he *used* the Jewish culture. He participated.

Luke 4:16: Jesus read the Torah, or the Old Testament books of Moses, and waited to give interpretation. He *used* the Jewish culture (dialogue).

Luke 5:3: As a teacher, He sat while teaching. He *used* culture (respect).

Luke 5:13: Jesus touched unclean lepers. He *rejected* the prevailing cultural view (out of universal love).

Luke 5:14: He healed a leper and showed the leper to the priest and with an offering. He *used* it (honored culture).

Luke 5:29: Unlike Jesus, Jewish leaders never ate with sinners and tax collectors. He *transformed* the culture.

Luke 5:33: Pharisees fasted to be seen by others, but Jesus called us to fast for the right motivation. He *transformed* culture.

Luke 19:45, 46: The Gentile room in the temple was used for animal sales. He *rejected* the culture.

Note that the culture and the religion were interlinked. This is exactly the situation with Muslim religion and Muslim culture.

Do Muslims pray? Yes. Do they pray at mealtimes or for God to heal them and to humble their hearts? No. We can transform their cultural features.

Think of transforming, using, and rejecting certain Muslim cultural features for the sake of removing "doors of resistance" in Islam.

3. Hero worship. Did you know that *you could revere a person or a (Muslim) people group and become so casual with them that the Gospel is never preached?* In 2 Corinthians 5:16, Paul said, "So from now on we regard no one from a worldly point of view. Though we once regarded Christ in this way, we do so no longer." We have found from experience that we don't want to be just "sweet" to Muslims. The heart of God for them doesn't consist simply of an honoring of their culture. Go beyond neighborliness alone.

In Matthew 10:37, Jesus said it this way: "Anyone who loves his father or mother more than me is not worthy of me; anyone who loves his son or daughter more than me is not worthy of me." When His mother called for Him, He asked in Matthew 12:48–50, "'Who is my mother, and who are my brothers?' Pointing to his disciples, he said, 'Here are my mother and my brothers. For whoever does the will of my Father in heaven is my brother and sister and mother.'"

Was Jesus too strict? Did he ignore the call to be humanitarian and pluralistic that is so prevalent today? No—just the opposite.

Note that Jesus's mother, Mary, was present at the cross and later in the upper room, and she was there during the movement of God at Pentecost. Putting God first really works! Bless people by keeping true to the vision of church planting.

Paul's word challenges "people preference," or idolatry of any kind. See Colossians 3:11: "Here there is no Greek or Jew, circumcised or uncircumcised, barbarian, Scythian, slave or free, but Christ is all, and is in all." We want to love Muslims whether they come to Christ or not. Such is unconditional love. *However, Christ must never be hidden from Muslims in order to better smooth out a relationship.* Doors of resistance to reaching Muslims can be of our own making.

Challenge: The Scriptures affirm the blessing of God upon Ishmael and upon his offspring. However, never do the Scriptures promise a blessing without intending that the fire of that blessing to light other peoples with the glory of God. Genesis 12:3 states that the blessing of God must be given away to others.

Question: Paul said, "However, as it is written: 'No eye has seen, no ear has heard, no mind has conceived what God has prepared for those who love Him.'" Ishmael means "God hears." Will we see those promises of God fulfilled in the offspring of Ishmael? Will we gain insight from the offspring of Ishmael as Muslims find the promise of God in Christ?

Case Study 9
Hyaat, a Muslim Friend
Whom God Loves

One Sunday, we welcomed to our ex-Muslim church in Paris a couple who had given their lives to Jesus Christ only one week before. Here is the story of Hyaat, the wife.

Hyaat was beaten and abused by her husband for years, until she finally did something few Muslim women do: she divorced him. Divorce in that part of the world carries the "luster of a dog," as they say in Algeria. So when Hyaat divorced, she tried to flee Algeria. However, without the permission of her divorced husband, she was not permitted to leave the country. Such are the laws. So instead, she traveled from town to town with her two children, finally living outside the desert city of Tamanrasset among the Tuareg nomads.

There, she found herself surrounded by a thousand men on camelback. (These were Hyaat's words. Remember that the Eastern person's description is permeated with the emotion, the image, and the power of the moment, not exactitude. The Hellenistic or Western way of describing an encounter with men on camelback is to describe not the emotional enormity, but rather exact details of, for example, forty-three scary men on camelback.) The expectation that Hyaat had was rape, subjugation, slavery, and severe abuse on a continual basis.

But instead, she and her two children somehow found respect in this incredible world of Sahara dwellers. A man from the Sahara village pitied her and stood in for her husband so Hyaat could be granted an exit visa to leave Algeria. The visa was granted.

She flew out on the next flight for Paris. Paris was no picnic, but it was better than Islamic Algeria, which to her meant fear and danger. While in Paris she met Patrick, an Italian who had lost his wife te years ago. Both Hyaat and Patrick met Mooloc an Algerian Muslim-background believer from church.

The couple became fascinated with the l God and came to our church; this was th time they had ever attended a church. Th changed when I asked for a volunteer to morning Scripture. Hyaat ran forward and read the Scripture with passion. I didn't realize that Hyaat was still a Muslim woman until after she read the verses. A Muslim read God's Word for me before the church! She had such a conviction of the Word. The Word of God that she read never left her heart. We led her to Christ that very morning. That Sunday, Hyaat and Patrick came to church for their first time and left committed to Christ.

Questions for the Reader

1. Muslims memorize the Bible verses that you read to them. What questions would you ask a Muslim after he or she recites a Bible story back to you?

2. Muslims must not whistle or sleep on their left side in bed or go to the bathroom with their left foot first. Jacob and Esau bartered over sheep with the most spots that changed magically. Elijah allowed Naaman to take some earth from Israel after he was healed by God. Where would you start with a Muslim seeker of Jesus with these strange beliefs?

CHAPTER 11

A Tool Kit for Getting Started

L et's look at some important tools in our tool kit. Why do we need tools? Practical issues will make or break our ministry to Muslims. We have had guests who felt that someone who ministered to Muslims didn't need knowledge of the Muslim culture. Others felt that God's Word was so universal that it didn't require team ministry. Still others gave Muslims only a godly example without interacting with them. Essential ministry needs, at the very least, some of the tools listed below.

Start with Prayer

We have observed Christian brothers in Niger and Chad who came from a non-Muslim, Christian background. These brothers were extremely effective in working among Muslims, even though they didn't have the Muslim cultural background. So what was their secret? Much prayer and cultural adaptation. For example, William didn't have a Muslim cultural or religious background as he worked in Chad. However, he spoke the local language and dressed in a billowing white robe to honor and to identify with the culture. He showed the love of God by helping new converts to raise cows and chickens. William honored the Muslim culture by meeting with the local council leaders, by gathering Muslims and various Muslim-background believers (MBBs) into groups that never looked Western. It was all part of his strategy to honor the culture and the local customs so that new converts would be able to relate the Gospel back to their families and villages for Christ.

Work in Teams

Work in teams, not individually. This is a golden rule. We, too, have tried to work without a team, only to find that the work is slow and hard because we don't have all the spiritual ministries that are found when many team members cooperate. *Also, a team is a minicommunity that mirrors the house groups or churches that we hope to plant.* It is easier to be encouraged with the added energy that is found in team ministry. One-on-one evangelism and discipleship should involve every team member, whether the individuals are evangelists, pastors, administrators, or mercy-minded team members. And be willing to give team members responsibilities of their own: trust new, young leaders, and give them early ownership. Let your team thrive with creativity.

Remember the Goal

Plant churches or groups among Muslims, rather than a random conversion here and there. The goal is more than just one person converted to Christianity in an isolated way. The goal should be reproducing leaders to build gatherings, churches, and even church-planting movements to encompass the very heart and life of Jesus Christ. In doing so, build churches as culturally relevant transformation communities, not just a place to attend a service. Muslim convert fellowships should be eager to reach out to others and to expand their numbers. Remember, *our approach is not mechanistic, but we are looking for ways to multiply the work of harvesting, sending, and resending more workers for results that are measurable.*

Teach MBBs to Accept Muslims

Conversion is not an excuse to form a club that rejects other Muslims. Many Muslim converts become anti-Muslim instead of committed to loving their Muslim friends and family. Teach and show MBBs to love other Muslims just as you do. Also, Muslim converts sometimes reject new Muslim converts. Due to the high price that most Muslims pay (which, however, is nothing compared to the price that Jesus paid), the tendency is for them to set the bar very high for new converts. This can lead to harshness as Muslim converts deal with other new Muslim converts. MBBs should love and encourage new converts who are weak or sinful in some area instead of rejecting them.

Teach MBBs to Accept Muslim Culture

Instead of letting Muslims despise the elements of their culture or past, help them produce creative worship that honors God through their unique cultural expression. Some Muslim convert fellowships actually ban worship in their former language. This is unnecessary, though, because Jesus Christ loves cultures and uses them to redeem both the people and the cultures themselves unto Himself. You can help MBBs by showing the example: identify with the Muslim community by taking on the same cultural norms yourself.

Prepare for Persecution

Someone once asked me if any member of our MBB fellowship had been persecuted. I replied that I didn't know of any who hadn't been persecuted.

It is important to prepare your MBBs for persecution, as Paul prepared many early Christians. Paul's first mentor, Ananias, was afraid of Paul because he had a reputation for violently persecuting Christians before he came to the Lord. But the Lord explained, "I will show him [Paul] how much he must suffer for the sake of My Name" (Acts 9:16). Paul even prepared Timothy for persecution: "Indeed all who desire to live a godly life in Christ Jesus will be persecuted" (2 Tim. 3:12). Paul prepared his followers for persecution by his own example. When Agabus prophesied that Paul would be bound and persecuted, the new disciples begged Paul to avoid Jerusalem. Paul asked the minichurch to stop weeping and breaking his heart, because he was ready to die for Jesus Christ (Acts 21:13).

We as church planters sometimes come from an individualized context. *Muslims live in community-centric cultures.* As church planters, we need to make a major adjustment so that we promote public gatherings, public reading of the Word, and baptisms in the presence of existing social networks.

How do you get started? Prepare Muslims to be carriers of the Gospel even before they are fully aware of the full implications of Jesus Christ as Lord.

Establish gatherings. Think in terms of public meetings. Let fellow seekers meet one another and form a small group of Muslim seekers. Team members, assigned according to their gifts and skills, should all be involved in intercession or at least within the scope of an accountability group. *Find out where God is at work, and join Him in that work.*

Your new Muslim convert fellowship or MBB gathering should emphasize the words of Jesus, His ways, His worth, and His life.

Challenge: The call of God to Abraham was a new concept of a Gospel that was to be portable (believers could go with the Gospel) and reproducible (others would respond to the call); it was to be a sort of public demonstration to the nations.

Question: How would the Gospel be shut off and stymied in a public proclamation among Muslim converts if they rejected their own Muslim cultural heritage and demonized their own cultural practices?

Case Study 10
Bedja, a Muslim Friend
Whom God Loves

When I was spreading the Gospel in Algeria, I received a letter from an MBB that read as follows:

"Hello, my name is Bedja. I am Algerian. Have you ever felt left and abandoned? I have. Before my conversion I knew my Koran. I was a devout Muslim. By the time that Algeria won independence from France, each and every missionary and every member of my church in Algiers just left Algeria. They all went to France or back to the USA.

"Then letters poured in from overseas. My friends begged me to 'escape' from Algeria. But instead of leaving Algeria, I just moved from Algiers to Constantine, still in Algeria. I felt I didn't need to leave Algeria because I had fellow Kabyle Berber friends in Constantine who would shelter me, and Constantine was safer than Algiers. Also the Lord told me that I wasn't abandoned. I had to trust God.

"Then one day, very quietly, a man came to my apartment in Constantine to drop off some mail. He asked me if he could have all his mail directed to my apartment address. I just stared at him, with my eyes focusing on his. Why would this man, one year before the year of Algerian independence, come to my apartment and ask me for permission to use my address?

"Somehow, I still agreed. After some weeks, he came to pick up his mail. One large envelope fell open. Out fell some Bible study materials that he had mailed to my address, obviously to avoid the legal implications of being caught with these materials at his address. I said to him, 'Brother, don't be afraid. I am a Christian, too. Why don't we pray together?' This was the beginning of our first cell group in Constantine. God did this.

"Shortly after meeting the man with the 'change of address,' I met a blind man who asked me for a Bible. He gave me an address. In those days the Braille Bible was big, like a thick bale of paper. So instead, I decided to just give him a Gospel of Luke in Braille.

"I went to his apartment, and I slowly walked up the dusty stairs to deliver the book. When the door opened, the blind man asked me in. To my shock and praise to God, Rachid the blind man had a group of nine that he was leading in his apartment. All were Christian converts from Islam. All wanted to study God's Word. Rachid had called eight of these people to Jesus Christ. I joined their Bible study. This was my first time in a Bible study.

"We had our second prayer and Bible cell group during a dangerous period just before Algeria's independence. During a time of intercession, I cried out to God because I had thought I was the only Christian in Constantine, Algeria. God told me this from Acts 18:9–10: 'And the Lord said to Paul one night in a vision, "Do not be afraid, but speak and do not be silent; for I am with you, and no man shall attack you to harm you; for I have many people in this city.'"

"In 1967, five years after Algeria's independence, I moved back to Algiers. My husband found work there, and it was calming down with slightly less fear and violence in the streets. Again I cried out to God, because Algiers was more closed than Constantine. God gave me the encouragement that I needed. He showed me that the earth was without form and void just before He created life (the book of Genesis). He showed me that in the same way, Algeria was without form and void, and now He would create His life in Algeria. Finally, He showed me that Algeria was like, even shaped like, a huge rock. God showed me that 'upon this rock' will the Lord build His church, just like He said to Peter: 'Upon the rock of this confession will I build my church.' He showed me that the rock of Algeria, upon this dusty dry rock of a nation, will the Lord build His church all across North Africa.

"I don't search for signs. But I want to see God's people in the hollow of God's hand, being born from God even as the earth was without form and void. Casbyr was God's open door to me. He rode an old bicycle all over the city of Algiers. His only task was to ask people to help deliver portions of the Bible, mostly Gospels of Luke. He knew the believers and met their Bible needs. Casbyr rode a rattling bike in the will of God, encouraging people like me. Casbyr was like the flow of the life of Christ through the arteries of His people who still stayed behind in Algeria.

"More encouragement followed. Small groups of believers, converts from Islam, would meet in my home. But one day, a fiery boldness and passion for Jesus fell on one of our groups of ten people soon after they met in secret in the snowy mountains of the Grand Kabyle. Noise came from the rest house because a local football team had an emergency. One of the team members had a perforated ulcer. The football team, all Kabyle Berbers, came running out of that rest house in search of a doctor. They met our small group of believers who were essentially 'in hiding.' The footballer was becoming unconscious with pain.

"Because medicine wasn't available, all our small group had to offer was prayer. We prayed in the name of Jesus Christ, and healing flooded down from heaven. Karem was instantly healed! The whole soccer team cried out to God, 'Allah, Allah.' They gave their lives to Jesus Christ on the spot. Every member of the team was saved. Now the news was out. The flame of Jesus Christ spread all over Kabylia."

Questions for the Reader

1. Would you allow your son or daughter to stay a month with a Muslim family in light of their hospitality?

2. Can a Muslim follower of Jesus continue attending the mosque?

CHAPTER 12

Practical Details

How do you get started?

Communicate the Gospel in terms and expressions that make sense to Muslims. Tell stories as you meet regularly for Bible study and discussion. Let them restate and recite the story you just told them, because we want the Word to be "mobile and transmissible." Prepare Muslims to be carriers of the Gospel even before they are fully aware of the full implications of Jesus Christ as Lord.

Serve and pray for the Muslim who is poor or sick. Establish gatherings. Think in terms of public meetings. Work in teams. One-on-one evangelism and discipleship should involve every team member, whether the individuals are evangelists, gifted as pastors, administrators, or mercy-minded team members. Find out where God is at work and join Him in that work.

Constantly talk about Jesus. Let fellow seekers meet one another and form a small group of

Muslim seekers. Establish gatherings. Team members, assigned according to their gifts and skills, should all be involved in intercession. Identify with the Muslim community by taking on the same cultural norms.

We as church planters sometimes come from an individualized context. *Muslims live in community-centric cultures.* We as church planters need to make a major adjustment so that we promote public gatherings, a public reading of the Word, and baptisms in the presence of existing social networks.

Again, prepare your Muslim-background believers (MBBs) for persecution as Paul did: "Sometimes you were publicly exposed to insult and persecution; at other times you stood side by side with those who were so treated" (Heb. 10:33).

Stories. What do I say to a Muslim? Tell him or her a story about how you met Jesus, or tell him or her the story of the lost son, the prodigal son from Luke 15. Prepare a three- to four-minute story. Write it out and practice it before a group of three of your friends.

Hospitality. Whom do you talk to? Find a man or woman of peace. Invite yourself to this person's home for tea, or invite him or her to your home for tea. If he or she drinks very sweet tea, join him or her; eat and drink whatever he or she offers you (Luke 10).

Diligence. Ask God to show you five Muslim people to hear your story this week. Take notes. Prayer opens the gates of heaven. Then tell your accountability group or team what happened. Ask for prayer. Work in a team, or at least within the scope of an accountability group.

Case Study 11
Nadia, a Muslim Friend
Whom God Loves

At six years old, Nadia cut herself loose from all Muslim tradition; she dared to be angry at God for judging her when she didn't go through the Muslim rite of washing before reading the Koran. She even took the risk of praying directly to God (Allah). She spoke to God! No Muslim should do this, but she did, even though she thought God might take her life as a punishment.

Then when Nadia was ten and was on a short trip to France, a woman approached her with some pictures. This missionary had flannel boards and wonderful stories of Jesus that blessed the heart of little Nadia. She would never forget the picture of the cross. Nor did she forget that missionary lady.

When she returned to her home in Oran, Algeria, she hungrily pored through the Koran for months to find out about God. However, she made

a huge mistake: she asked her father about incon-
sistencies in the Koran, things that were confus-
ing. Her father went ballistic, warning her never to
question the Koran.

One day, the faithful missionary Nadia had met
traveled to Algeria to link Nadia up with some
amazing missionaries in Oran. Nadia continued to
visit this missionary group, and soon the links were
forged between them. Time passed, and when
she was sixteen, Nadia was invited to a Christian
youth retreat in Algeria, which mingled Christian
and Muslim youth in a session that expounded the
glory of God and the cross of Jesus. Then, during
a walk through the forest on her own, Nadia asked
for Jesus to be her Lord.

After the retreat Nadia went home filled with
a new life, and she tried to meet other Christians
like her. News came that there was a forest nearby
where Christians met and worshiped God. Without
hesitating, she dashed out to meet these people.
She just loved the freedom in Jesus, the teaching,
the "like-mindedness" of the people, and the vision
they had about the Son of God.

However, trouble loomed ahead on Nadia's
path. Muslim secret-police officers were there in
the forest, posing as Christians so that they could
spy on new converts. Later, there was a knock at

the door of Nadia's family home, and the police demanded that Nadia go with them to the police headquarters for an interview. Nadia's mother, still unaware of Nadia's conversion, demanded to accompany her daughter. It was in the police station that the cards were laid on the table. Nadia's mother was crushed, and Nadia quickly became the object of scorn.

After this point, anyone could have murdered Nadia with impunity. Nadia basically lost her rights as a human being. At home the twenty-year-old Nadia was verbally abused, rejected, and beaten— again and again and again.

The events that followed were beyond strange. Nadia had found refuge in the Lord and in sharing Jesus with everyone she met. Normally, such evangelism would be met with a ticket to prison. But instead, the police, who knew that Christians were harmless, called Nadia in again only to advise her to proceed cautiously. They respected her and wanted her to survive. The second event was that her parents and siblings became more hardened and more committed to Islam than ever before.

Nadia lived in her home as a stranger. Family decisions were made, and family discussions took place, but Nadia was ignored as if she didn't belong to the family. To her family, Nadia was dead and buried.

One day an old friend who had not seen Nadia in three years came by for a visit. Even though Nadia was right there in the house, Nadia's mother opened the door and said, "Nadia is not here; she's dead. She died two years ago. Our family has grieved for her." Nadia was dead to her family.

Then Nadia remembered what she had read in the Bible: we must be crucified with Christ and die to our sins. Only then will we be truly alive, for then we will be made alive in Christ, raised up together with Him. She received the pronouncement "Nadia is dead" as Christ's affirmation of her life.

Later, Nadia was blessed with an opportunity to move to France. When she arrived, she embraced the missionary lady who had once showed her the "flannel cross." Today, Nadia is our worship leader.

Questions for the Reader

1. Muslims say that they would rather be dead than shamed. What do they mean by "shame"?

2. Western Christians are often private about their faith. Muslims are very public about their faith. How can a private Western Christian reach a public-minded Muslim? Is the answer to have the Muslim tell everyone about his or her conversion?

CHAPTER 13

Speak the Word

Rasina, a formerly Muslim woman, sent a fax from Kabylia, Algeria, to our church in Paris. She said, "I am converted to Jesus Christ. I think I am the only Christian in Algeria." Her cry for help was clear. She longed for a community of believers in Christ.

Chaffiq, a Tuareg nomad from Tamanrasset, Algeria, had a different story. He wrote to a radio station for more information on how to become a follower of Jesus Christ. We went to find him even though the only information we had about him was his post office–box number in southern Algeria. He sat down with us at a coffee bar. "I have two questions," Chaffiq started. "First of all, why is Jesus called the Son of God? Second, I asked for help three years ago. What took you so long to come to me?" "Son of..." is an Eastern language derivative that means the perfect likeness a person has to a certain character or trait.

Jesus is the Son of God. How can you tell Muslims right away?
Ibn a Heera: prostitute
Ibn Hamouni: son of my sorrows
Ibn Acroute: bad person
Sons of Encouragement
Sons of Thunder

Rasina and Chaffiq are examples of the need that Muslims and Muslim-background believers (MBBs) are facing today. It is time for us to realize this need among Muslims and carry on the vision that was handed to Abraham, the father of Ishmael and Isaac. With joy we read God's promise to both Abraham and to us, his descendants: "I will establish my covenant as an everlasting covenant between me and you and your descendants after you for the generations to come, to be your God and the God of your descendants after you" (Gen. 17:7).

In the following verse, we can read about the specific vision passed on to us for the Muslim world: "The whole land of Canaan, where you are now an alien, I will give as an everlasting possession to you and your descendants after you; and I will be their God" (Gen. 17:8). Canaan corresponds to present-day Israel/Palestine and parts of Jordan, Syria, Lebanon, and Turkey.

And we can read the vision God passed on to us for the rest of the Muslim world in the Middle East: "On that day the Lord made a covenant with Abram and said, 'To your descendants I give this land, from the river of Egypt to the great river, the Euphrates— the land of the Kenites, Kenizzites, Kadmonites, Hittites, Perizzites, Rephaites, Amorites, Canaanites, Girgashites and Jebusites'" (Gen. 15:18–21).

Having a vision for Muslim evangelism and the building of MBB transformational communities is the work of God but also a blessing for us! Imagine the joy of entering a shame-and-honor community, taking away some of the obstacles from your own cultural ideas, and seeing the work of God flowering before your eyes. My point here is that we Westerners can mutually profit from these transformational communities. Let's share the vision.

And let us not forget the example of our ultimate mentor, Jesus Himself, who also shared this vision: "And the Word became flesh and dwelt among us, full of grace and truth; we have beheld his glory, glory as of the only Son from the Father" (John 1:14). "Becoming flesh" was not just an exercise of endowing Himself with skin and blood— Jesus wrapping Himself with culture and taking on our grief and sorrow. He came to dwell with us, not just to visit us.

Every language and culture and members of all the peoples of the earth will gather around the throne of God and worship the Lamb. My prayer is the prayer of Abraham: "And Abraham said unto God, O that Ishmael might live before thee!" (Gen. 17:18). May every Muslim group you encounter live before God.

Be encouraged, all of God's people who are ready to take the challenge to "speak the Word of God without fear" (Phil. 1:14). The Lord Himself said in Ezekiel 12:25, "I will speak the word and perform it, says the Lord GOD." Speak the Word.

Challenge: Jesus's Great Commission was that the disciples should go forth and preach the Gospel to all nations. Long before this, Abraham made a similar statement about the Ishmaelites when he told God, "O that Ishmael might live before you!" The Tower of Babel experiment in Genesis produced the opposite result in that it divided all nations and peoples. It was not the subduing shalom peace of God that would cover the world with God's truth and His love. Babel was introversion in the face of God's call to subdue the earth.

Question: How can born-again shame-and-honor communities of Muslim converts expand and purify my own life in God and better prepare me to live in the community of the King on earth?

Case Study 12
Asmaa, a Muslim Friend
Whom God Loves

I will never forget the way that I wrote down the page number of the Gospel of Luke so she could find the story of the prodigal son.

I didn't want to defile the Word of God to a Muslim by writing in the Bible. The passion of trying to find a way to tell her about God and yet honor her culture was unforgettable. Here's Asmaa's story.

Asmaa was thrilled to hear a Bible story. I told her I was taking a risk, partly because I was standing out in the middle of the street and especially because I was within sight of her father, mother, sisters, and brothers. She said it was just great to talk about a Bible story. I was mostly afraid that by underlining the Bible verse that she would think I was defiling the Bible. (Muslims also consider the Bible as a holy book.) She knew she could trust our family, because we had already given them a worship CD in Arabic and French. Her promise to me was that she would definitely read the story of the prodigal son. Then my conscience pricked me again. I remembered that Muslims are part of an oral culture. It just never crossed my mind that I should have recited the story to her.

Remember that Muslims are part of an oral culture, whether they are literate or illiterate. What does this mean? It means that even literate Muslims receive heartfelt truth through the telling of stories. Lists and printed pages are Western. Parables, sayings, repetition, and recitations of stories are Eastern and hence well suited to Muslims. True, some Muslims are converted by reading the Gospel of Luke. However, the majority of Muslims who become Christians are able to communicate the Gospel best to their family and friends through storytelling. It should come as no surprise that oral peoples are also capable of memorizing and retaining long and detailed stories with amazing accuracy. Imagine the value of the Gospel being woven into the fabric of whole Muslim villages, family legends, and the sayings along the dusty trail of the Sahara Desert of North Africa.

Questions for the Reader

1. What do you say to a Muslim convert who still locks his wife in the bedroom?

2. When a Muslim becomes a follower of Jesus, would you encourage him to fast during Ramadan to identify with other Muslims?

3. A Muslim husband may be a converted Muslim but might not tell his Muslim wife for fifteen years after his conversion. Why?

4. How can Muslim converts lead Westerners to Christ? Is it possible?

Every language and culture and members of all the peoples of the earth will gather around the throne of God and worship the Lamb! My prayer is the prayer of Abraham: "And Abraham said unto God, O that Ishmael might live before thee!" (Gen. 17:18). For every Muslim group you encounter, may they live before God!

Be encouraged, all of God's people who are ready to take the challenge to "speak the Word of God without fear" (Phil. 1:14). The Lord Himself said in Ezekiel 12:25, "I will speak the word and perform it, says the Lord GOD." Speak the Word!

In Ghana, Don Heckman was brought to Christ through the witness of his physics and math students. While spending time in prayer in a remote African village, Don felt God's call to French ministries in a cross-cultural context.

Beginning in 1971, Don and his wife, Evey, served first as missionaries in Europe, where they developed eight disciple-training centers; then in

Eastern Europe during the communist years, when they formed a literature outreach program; and also in North and West Africa, where they reached out through evangelistic ministry. Evey has worked in Afghanistan, Albania, Ethiopia, and across East Africa. From 1990 to 1997, Don and Evey planted a bilingual French/English church, a Tamil church for Sri Lankans, two French churches, and finally a church for Muslim-background believers, all in Paris, the first of its kind in all of France.

Don received his MDiv and his ThM in missiology from Fuller Seminary. Don and Evey have been married for thirty-one years. Don travels into North African and Middle Eastern countries, mentoring teams, mobilizing new workers, and encouraging church planting in ethnic contexts.

For additional copies of this book or for speaking requests, mobilizing, mentoring, or coaching, send an e-mail to hdonparis@gmail.com. Contact Amazon.com for more books as gifts, study books for gatherings of any size, or Kindle and e-books.

About this Book

Don Heckman is the author of this book, available on Amazon as soft cover, kindle or e-book. Not a "how to" book, this book is filled with ways to enter into another culture and world view, and a legacy of real time memoirs that Don experienced and recorded to reconcile Muslims to Christians.

I was inspired to write this book from experiences I've had, really memoirs, of my association with Muslim people. This took place over a period of 30 years, as I took on the joy of reconciling Muslims not with the Western Culture, but with Christ. I learned that the secret was listening to their stories, their needs and action filled parts of what they call The Religion.

Reconciliation requires time to listen to Muslims. There is no shortcut to listening. Also, knowing and becoming part of their Eastern worldview creates acceptance, regardless of my Western background. A Western world view is easily viewed as spirituality like a postage stamp on an envelope in terms of religious and non-religious involvement. The Eastern world view is the complete envelope. That is, issues of banking, relationships, church or mosque attendance, hospitality, schooling and just every aspect of life is under the worldview of Islam. We compartmentalize. They "envelope," pardon the pun.

Muslims can become Jesus followers without going through the confessional process of Western Christianity. We talk to Westerners who become Jesus-followers, which is valid, that is, for people to call on the name of the Lord with a Christian message.

Muslims have a phrase that they recite to become Muslims. It is called the "Shahada." But following their worldview involves internal and mostly external changes of allegiance. New Muslim "converts" may burn talisman and witchcraft objects as they associate with other followers of Jesus and even to weep and cry for dreams and revelation from God. They cherish baptism as they become followers of Jesus.

So for a Westerner to seek out Muslims to become Jesus followers, put away creeds, lists of things to do and not do, and preaching topics. Rather, let them read the Bible and discuss what the Bible passage says to them about who Jesus/Isa or God wants of them. Let them discover. These Eastern people of "wisdom" need to ruminate over concepts. Westerners must not be surprised if Muslims find new or conflicting theological ideas. Whether they are literate or illiterate, they love stories which they memorize nearly word for word. Remember: It's not lists, but stories.

Two key avenues to find reconciliation with Muslims are first to know that they treasure hospitality as part of their religo-cultural view toward people, probably more than you may imagine. So invite them and eat with them. But another avenue of pristine importance is to call yourself a "hanifi" follower of Jesus. This means you have the faith of Abraham, which they all strive but fail to have. Open these doors. This book opens us to Muslims that I personally know and who have come to know Jesus as a true follower of our Lord.

What God has done in our place of ministry: Our ministry is, in part, to nearby Muslims. This year we were blessed to have a desert camel-riding nomad called a Tuareg in our home. We read the story of Jesus healing the blind man in French to Maouli, a 38 year old who has never been in school for even a day and is completely illiterate. So I asked him to recite back to me the story of Jesus and the blind man. He memorized the story, word for word. We asked him what the story tells him about Jesus. The conversation went into the heart of Jesus from that point on. His words, "If we are patient and call upon Jesus/Isa, He will heal us."

What We Do:

1. Weekly visits to the local market is our outreach to countless Muslims, Evey my wife works with women and Don with men. We invite Muslims to our home, try to also get to their homes, and to build bridges to Christ through weekly and market place visits. One mother, very young, came running up to Evey for the 3rd time, just to open her heart and life to Evey.

2. My Mission commission is to train leaders of the various Algerian people groups and to train the France-based former Muslim group leaders. To do this, I preach in churches and groups which, some of them, are spin offs from the Muslim Background church we

planted in Paris. I meet with people who are such leaders in order to train them.

3. Part of my commission is to meet with my Mission and other missionary leaders. We met with prospective high level and tested leaders to move them to Algeria. We sent off one couple and their two children last month to live in Algeria. My recruiting and training has sent a family of 5 to work among Muslims in India. This family is considered such a key leader now that church leaders in India are swarming with the now accomplished family in New Deli.

4. I have been a peace keeper among Muslim Background Believer organizations in France. Peace making is possible with my experience and the Lord's hand on my life to apply Coaching principles to bring out the best of goal attainment to all the missionary Muslim organizations. In Malta, at the North Africa Partnership, the 400 attendees voted me as part of the organizational steering committee. The trust in us is there, because we are not sectarian and with no axe to grind, but rather to love and strengthen relationships with leaders across Algeria and France.

Evey has assisted the Muslim Background women's gathering of 80 women and made it possible for many of the attendees to function as redeemed Christian women, after having been beaten to a pulp by their Muslim husbands. These women are taught that it is part of being a good Muslim to accept the daily beatings

Pray for us to rescue and "adopt" the broken men and women of Islam, not by being superior, but by empowering them to consider Jesus Christ as redeemer and way-maker.

Join us in Prayer and ministry to help convey the Life in Jesus who makes all things and people new.